The Matrix of the Mind

The Matrix of the Mind

Object Relations and
the Psychoanalytic Dialogue

Thomas H. Ogden, M.D.

Jason Aronson Inc.
Northvale, New Jersey
London

Library of Congress Cataloging-in-Publication Data

Ogden, Thomas H.
  The matrix of the mind

  Bibliography: p.247
  Includes index.
  1. Object relations (Psychoanalysis)   2. Mother
and child.   3. Mental illness.   I. Title.
BF175.0365   1986   616.89   85-13404
ISBN 0-87668-742-7

Certain chapters of this volume are based on prior publications of the author, as follows: *Chapter 2*: "Instinct, phantasy and psychological deep structure: a reinterpretation of aspects of the work of Melanie Klein," *Contemporary Psychoanalysis* 20:500–525, 1984; *Chapter 6*: "The concept of internal object relations," *International Journal of Psycho-Analysis* 64:181–198, 1983; *Chapter 7*: "The mother, the infant, and the matrix: interpretations of aspects of the work of Donald Winnicott," *Contemporary Psychoanalysis*, 21:346–371, 1985; *Chapter 8*: "On potential space," *International Journal of Psycho-Analysis* 66:129–141, 1985.

To my wife, Sandra

Contents

7

The Mother, the Infant, and the Matrix in the Work of Donald Winnicott   167

8

Potential Space   203

9

Dream Space and Analytic Space   233

Acknowledgments

I would like to express my gratitude to my wife, Sandra, whose insight into the ideas I have been developing has been indispensable in the writing of this book.

Clinical and theoretical discussions with Dr. James Grotstein have formed an important background for many of the concepts presented in this volume. I am deeply indebted to him for the warmth and generosity he has shown me as a friend and teacher.

I am grateful to Dr. Bryce Boyer for all that he has taught me about the art, the discipline, and the courage involved in treating very disturbed patients. The seminars I have taught with him have been a great source of pleasure for me.

As will become clear in the course of this book, I believe that ideas are formed and developed dialectically. I am indebted to the supervisees with whom I have worked, and the members of the various seminars that I have led on object relations theory, for helping to create a series of generative dialogues that shaped the ideas discussed in this volume.

Thomas H. Ogden, M.D.

The Matrix of the Mind

1

The Psychoanalytic Dialogue

We die with the dying:
See, they depart, and we go with them.
We are born with the dead:
See, they return, and bring us with them.

—T. S. Eliot, Four Quartets

This book is offered as an act of interpretation. Different psychoanalytic perspectives are much like different languages. Despite the extensive overlap of semantic content of the written texts of different languages, each language creates meaning that cannot be generated by the other languages now spoken or preserved in written form. The interpreter is not merely a passive carrier of information from one person to another; he is the active preserver and creator of meaning as well as the retriever of the alienated. As such, the interpreter safeguards the fullness of human discourse.

Psychoanalysis, both as a therapeutic process and as a set of ideas, develops in the form of a discourse between

1

subjects, each interpreting his own productions and those
of the other. Speaking for the moment about psychoanalysis as a theory (or, more accurately, a set of theories),
each important contribution provides a degree of resolution for a theoretical or clinical problem, and in so doing
creates a new epistemologic dilemma. A subsequent contribution no longer addresses the same issue that an earlier contribution has addressed, for that problem no longer
exists; it has been forever altered. The more significant
the contribution, the more radically (and interestingly)
the epistemologic problem is transformed.

British object relations theory represents a diverse
collection of contributions to the psychoanalytic discourse and has altered the character of the epistemologic
problems presently accessible for psychoanalytic consideration. In this volume several pivotal ideas emerging from
the work of the British school will be discussed, primarily
concepts introduced by Melanie Klein, Donald Winnicott,
and, in a more limited way, Ronald Fairbairn and Wilfred
Bion. I do not attempt to survey or synthesize the contributions of these analysts; rather, my aim is to clarify,
critique, and interpret, and in the process to generate new
analytic understandings. Even though I will discuss individual concepts and groups of concepts contributed by
members of the British school, I hope to convey something of the movement of thought underlying the unusu-
ally generative discourse in which these ideas were developed. The contributions to the psychoanalytic dialogue
upon which I will focus were made in the period between
1925 and the early 1970s. That discourse is over, and I will
not attempt to reconstruct it historically. My rendering of
Klein, Winnicott, Fairbairn, Bion, and others is not an
effort to replicate the thinking of these analysts, since the
moment in the dialogue at which their contributions were

made has passed. All that can be alive at present is our own capacity for interpretation, and it is toward that end that I will devote my efforts.

Both in the analytic dialogue (between analyst and analysand) and in the psychoanalytic discourse (among analytic thinkers), each act of intepretation preserves the original (experience or idea) while simultaneously generating new meanings and understandings of oneself and the other. Unless the original is preserved through language and in conscious and unconscious memory, we are trapped in a never-ending present upon which we cannot reflect and from which we cannot learn. The isolation of a portion of either the analytic dialogue between patient and analysand, or the analytic discourse among analytic thinkers results in individual or cultural self-alienation. It is not that a part of the past disappears; that cannot happen, because the past is immutable. We can, however, isolate ourselves from our history. History differs from the past in that the past is simply a collection of events, while history is a creation reflecting our conscious and unconscious memory of, our personal and collective rendering of, our distortions of, our interpretations of, the past. By isolating ourselves from the history of the dialogue that has preceded us and, in a sense, has created us in the present, we become less able to recognize and understand ourselves fully through the symbols, the meanings, the ideas, the feelings, the art, and the work that we create. To the extent that we isolate ourselves from a portion of the discourse, we are deadened, because to that same degree, we do not exist for ourselves (i.e., self-reflectively). A principal goal of clinical psychoanalysis is the progressive recapturing of self-alienated personal experience, isolated from the intrapersonal and interpersonal discourse, a process that allows the analysand to more fully recognize and understand who he is, and who he is becoming. In the retrieval of the alienated, the analysand becomes more fully alive as a subjective, historical human being. He becomes more capable of engaging in a fuller (less self-alienated) intrapersonal as well as interpersonal dialogue. He becomes less fearful of that which he formerly isolated from himself and, to that extent, becomes more free.

My goal in the present volume is to contribute to the retrieval of the alienated through my own acts of interpretation of ideas introduced by Klein, Winnicott, Fairbairn, and Bion. The contributions of these analysts to a large extent have been isolated from the worldwide psychoanalytic dialogue, leading to a depleting form of self-alienation in psychoanalytic thinking (see Jacoby [1983] for a discussion of the ahistorical character of American psychoanalysis over the past forty years).

The first portion of this volume re-interprets facets of the work of Melanie Klein. In the initial chapter on Klein (Chapter 2), a study of the Kleinian conception of phantasy is used as a vehicle for exploring psychoanalytic instinct theory as a theory of meaning. I will propose that Chomsky's concept of linguistic deep structure provides a useful analog for the understanding of the Kleinian conception of "phylogenetic inheritance of ideas." Instinct theory is viewed not as a theory of inherited, preformed ideas but, rather, as a theory of inborn, organizing codes (associated with the life and death instincts) by which perception is organized and meanings are attached to experience in a highly determined way.

A reinterpretation of Kleinian instinct theory serves to provide a fresh understanding of the monumental significance of Freud's instinct theory. Freud's contribution is not a static text but, rather, a set of ideas that is constantly evolving and being transformed in the context of the subsequent dialogue. We take it for granted that one cannot understand Klein without understanding Freud; I believe that it is also true that one cannot fully understand Freud without understanding Klein. Freud was aware that his writing contained more meaning than he himself recognized. It was for this reason that he rarely revised his earlier papers; rather, he allowed them to stand as they were and added ideas he developed later in the form of footnotes to the original text. In that way, he hoped to avoid inadvertently obfuscating the truth of the earlier version, which he was concerned he would lose as his thinking "progressed."

Kleinian theory dwells heavily on the nature of primitive mental contents, but this most explicit level of Klein's thinking often obscures the implicit theory of biological structure as the organizing container for the ideational and affective contents of mind. In Chapters 3, 4, and 5, the Kleinian conceptions of the paranoid-schizoid and depressive positions are interpreted as conceptions of states of being. Entry into these positions represents the transition from the purely biological to psychological experience (the paranoid-schizoid position) and from the impersonal-psychological to subjective experience (the depressive position). The distinctive states of being associated with each of these positions together (in a dialectical interplay similar to that between the conscious and unconscious mind, but not divided along lines of consciousness) constitute enduring, fundamental components of all subsequent psychological states.

A series of clinical vignettes is presented in Chapter 5 that focus upon patients who are involved in making a transition from a predominantly paranoid-schizoid mode of organizing experience to a depressive mode of organizing experience. It is of central clinical importance that the therapist be able to recognize and understand the nature of this transition, since his understanding of this shift in the patient's mode of organizing experience powerfully influences the way the therapist listens, how he intervenes, and how he understands the patient's response to his intervention.

In Chapter 6, the development of the concept of internal object relations is traced through the work of Freud, Abraham, Klein, Fairbairn, Winnicott, and Bion. Fairbairn's revision of Freud and Klein constitutes a critical advance in the development of object relations theory. I propose in this chapter that internal object relations be thought of as paired, split-off, and repressed aspects of ego. These paired aspects of self (the internal object relationship) are viewed not simply as self and object representations, but as paired suborganizations of personality capable of semi-autonomously generating experience.

This discussion of the concept of internal object relations represents an exploration of one side—the object or content side—of a dialectical relationship between the container and the contained, a relationship between psychological-interpersonal space and its mental contents. As such, this chapter prepares the way for a study of the work of Donald Winnicott, whose work is devoted to the study of the other side—the container side—of this dialectical pair.

In the final three chapters, I seek to clarify, interpret, and extend aspects of the work of Donald Winnicott, including his conception of the development of the mother–infant. The work of both Freud and Klein focused on the nature of psychological contents, functions and structures and their intrapsychic and interpersonal (e.g., transferential) manifestations. Winnicott expanded the field of psychoanalytic exploration to include a study of the development of the space in which mental contents, functions, and structures, as well as interpersonal relations, exist.

In Chapters 8 and 9, Winnicott's concept of potential space is discussed in terms of a series of dialectical relationships between reality and fantasy, me and not-me, symbol and symbolized, etc., each pole creating, preserving, and negating its opposite. This concept is perhaps the most important of Winnicott's contributions to psychoanalysis and at the same time the most elusive of his ideas. Potential space is not initially an intrapsychic space, for there is not yet an individual psyche in early infancy; rather, it is at first an interpersonal space created jointly by mother and infant. It is in this space that the individual infant "begins to be" (Winnicott, 1967a) and later learns to play, dream, work, and to create and interpret his symbols. Failure to create or maintain this dialectical process leads to forms of psychopathology that include the experiencing of one's thoughts, feelings, and perceptions as things in themselves; the foreclosure of imagination; fetishistic object usage; and a failure to attach meaning to experience.

Emerging from the dialogue that constitutes object relations theory are important contributions to a psychoanalytic conceptualization of mental contents (e.g., the concept of preconceptions of objects [psychological deep structure], the concept of internal object relations, the notion of the discovery of the externality of objects). But beyond this is the understanding developed in this portion of the psychoanalytic dialogue that mental contents exist in a psychological space that is at first almost entirely interpersonal, only later evolving into a personal internal environment. It is the dialectical interplay of our mental contents and the personal and interpersonal psychological space in which they are lived that constitutes the matrix of the mind.

2

Instinct, Phantasy, and Psychological Deep Structure in the Work of Melanie Klein

If you are applying psychoanalytic treatment to children you should meet Melanie Klein. . . . She is saying some things that may or may not be true, and you must find out for yourself for you will not get what Melanie Klein teaches in my analysis with you.

—*Communication by James Strachey to his analysand Donald Winnicott*

Although a significant proportion of the world's analysts are Kleinian analysts, a serious consideration of the work of Melanie Klein has not been a major part of the dialogue that constitutes American psychoanalytic thinking. Too often, when Klein's theory is considered, it is scrutinized only long enough to be dismissed on the basis of one

9

"untenable" idea or another, such as Klein's conception of the death instinct, her developmental timetable, or her theory of technique.

Although I am not a Kleinian and have profound disagreements with many aspects of her work, my aim is to present Klein's thinking in a light that may account for the important influence her ideas have had on the development of psychoanalytic thought outside the United States. In particular, Klein has had a powerful influence on the development of British object relations theory, as much through the rejection of her ideas as by their acceptance. The work of Winnicott, Fairbairn, Guntrip, and Balint must in large part be understood as a reaction to Kleinian theory. Klein's ideas and the reaction against them constitute a good deal of the dialogue underlying the development of object relations theory. The dynamics of this dialogue are incomprehensible if one has never embraced Klein's ideas for even a moment. One must understand Kleinian theory in order to move beyond it.

The Concept of Phantasy

In discussing Klein, one must begin with the concept of phantasy, for this is the hub of the mind–body system she envisions. Phantasy[1] for Klein (1952a) is the psychic

---

[1]English analysts, particularly the Kleinians, have tended to use the *ph* spelling of phantasy. Isaacs (1952) felt that the *ph* spelling connotes more of the unconscious dimension of the idea, whereas fantasy with an *f* should be used to refer to the more conscious, daydream level of this group of mental activities. Non-Kleinian, American analysts have never employed this distinction. Although Strachey in the Standard Edition uses the *ph* spelling of phantasy exclusively, American analysts have used only the *f* spelling. In this volume, I will use the spelling adopted by the analyst whose work is under discussion.

representation of instinct. Instinct itself is a biological entity, and so phantasy is the psychic representation of one's biology. Instinct must undergo some type of transformation in order to generate "mental corollaries" (Isaacs, 1952)—i.e., phantasies. The functional unit of the mind that is responsible for this transformation is the id. Instincts, as part of one's biology, are present from birth, and the id performs its transformational function from the beginning. The newborn infant's world at the outset is a bodily world, and phantasy represents the infant's attempt to transform somatic events into a mental form. Even into adulthood, phantasy never loses its connection with the body. Phantasy content is always ultimately traceable to thoughts and feelings about the workings and contents of one's own body in relation to the workings and contents of the body of the other.

Klein's conception of instinct derives from Freud's (1905) definition of instinct as "the demand made [by the body] upon the mind for work" (p. 168). For Klein, the body's "demand" has information encoded in it that the mind (specifically, the id) as receiver transforms into psychic phenomena with specific contents.

A great part of that which makes up one's inherited constitution appears on a psychological plane through the operation of the instincts. Does this mean that the infant inherits thoughts, and thinks those thoughts from the beginning? This would clearly be an untenable psychological theory. Unfortunately, it is very often at this juncture that Kleinian theory is dismissed as absurd. Many analysts see little point in pursuing a theory that evolves from the assumptions that the infant is born with ideas that do not derive from experience and that the infant can think at birth in ways that Piaget has shown are not possible until much later in development. Before discarding the whole system of Kleinian thought on these grounds, however, it

is worthwhile to listen carefully to the language of the
Kleinians to see if such apparently untenable ideas make
sense from any perspective.

In her classic paper on phantasy, Isaacs (1952)
writes,

> It has sometimes been suggested that unconscious
> phantasies such as that of "tearing [the breast] to
> bits" would not arise in the child's mind before he
> had gained the conscious knowledge that tearing a
> person to bits would mean killing him or her. Such a
> view does not meet the case. It overlooks the fact that
> such knowledge is *inherent* in bodily impulses as a
> vehicle of instinct, in the *aim* of instinct, in the
> excitation of the organ, i.e. in this case, the mouth.
>
> The phantasy that his passionate impulses will
> destroy the breast does not require the infant to have
> actually seen objects eaten up and destroyed, and
> then to have come to the conclusion that he could do
> it too. This aim, this relation to the object, is inherent
> in the character and direction of the impulse itself
> and in its related affects. (pp. 93–94)

Isaacs is proposing here that the idea of tearing an
object to bits is not learned but, rather, is intrinsic to the
aim of the instinct. Klein makes the same point when she
attributes the infant's knowledge of the breast before it
is encountered to "phylogenetic inheritance" (1952a,
p. 117 fn.). In this conception of instinct, the Kleinians have
expanded the concept of aim from Freud's (1905, 1915a)
original usage, in which the aim of an instinct was the
discharge of tension. Isaacs's usage is not incompatible
with Freud's but it goes beyond his to state that the aim of
the instinct in any given instance is characterized by a
specific type of object relatedness that includes specific

affective and ideational qualities not dependent on actual experience with objects.

Psychological Deep Structure

If the infant is not born with thoughts, how does he come by this "knowledge" of objects if not by experience? The Kleinians do not offer an answer to the question beyond the notion of "phylogenetic inheritance" (Klein, 1952c), but I believe that an answer might be provided by analogy with Chomsky's (1957, 1968) concept of linguistic deep structure. Infants are not born knowing French, English, Russian, or any other language, but given an ordinary environment and ordinary constitutional endowment, each infant learns at least one of the languages now spoken on this planet. It is simply not possible, according to Chomsky, for a human being to deduce and operational-ize the grammatical structure of language without a pre-existing system with which to select from and organize the mass of sounds to which one is exposed. Chomsky refers to this system, this code, as the "deep structure" of language. The individual does not have to, nor could he, create a grammar. The infant is born with a code that is built into the mode of functioning of his perceptual, cogni-tive, and motor apparatuses that will determine that he will organize sensory data and render them linguistically meaningful in a highly specific way. In other words, the infant will organize auditory stimuli in a way that is determined by the inborn code.

The assumption underlying Chomsky's concept of deep structure is that human beings do not randomly organize experience. Nothing is perceived absolutely freshly, i.e., free of preconceptions, preexisting schemata, preexisting systems for organizing that which is perceived.

Meaning cannot be generated absolutely *de novo*. Very similar understandings of the processing of experience in terms of inherent structures have been developed by Jakobson and de Saussure in the field of linguistics, Levi-Strauss in the field of anthropology, and Piaget in the field of developmental psychology.

To begin with a basic example of an inherent system of organizing perception, human color perception is not simply a matter of passively receiving sensory data and converting those data into visual experience. The primary colors, perceived as discrete differentiated groupings, are the products of a preexisting schema by which one organizes into groups certain portions of the continuous range of wavelengths of light (Bornstein, 1975). The groupings of wavelengths that we call colors are both arbitrary and universal among human beings and are the product of the way in which we organize the continuous spectrum of wavelengths, each wavelength differing from the next one by a fixed quantity of energy. We all divide the spectrum in precisely the same way (in the absence of color blindness) because of a preexisting biological schema that we use to organize our perceptions.

Similarly, our organization of sounds into phonemes (the basic units of sound from which words are constructed) is not a matter of passive reception of an existing external order. The distinction between the phonemes "ba" and "pa," for example, is not a quality of the stimuli themselves. Rather, it is built into our system of organizing stimuli. The human being is incapable of perceiving any sound as existing between these two phonemes (Eimas, 1975).

The shapes and shadings composing the human face are preferentially discernible by the infant on the basis of constitutionally determined modes of organizing perception (Stern, 1983). Again, we organize visual data into groupings (in this instance shapes and shadings) that are not our own individual creations but, rather, the product of a system for organizing perception that is shared by all human beings.

Inherited modes of organizing experience can be viewed as the counterpart of animal instincts. The chick has an inherited code with which to organize and respond to stimuli, a code that precedes any actual experience. The chick, without prior experience of predatory danger, will scurry for cover upon sighting the wing pattern of a predator (Lorenz, 1937; Tinbergen, 1957).

From the perspective of the concept of inherited codes or templates by which actual experience is organized, the Kleinian concept of inborn "knowledge . . . inherent in bodily impulses" (Isaacs, 1952, p. 94) can be understood not as inherited thoughts, but as a biological code that is an integral part of instinct. The infant is not born with the knowledge of, or phantasy about, tearing at the breast, but has a powerful predisposition to organize and make sense of experience along specific lines. Whether those predetermined lines are the ones proposed by Klein is still very much an open question. The conceptualization of instincts as psychological deep structures, however, seems a necessary addition to psychoanalytic instinct theory (Grotstein, 1985; Ogden, 1985). (See Samuels, 1983, for an application of a similar conception of "inheritance of knowledge" to the understanding of Jung's concept of archetypes.)

The Preconception and the Realization

In the beginning, phantasy is the infant's interpretation of experience. (I will defer a discussion of the form of symbolization and the degree of subjectivity that Klein attrib-

utes to the infant's experience at the beginning of development.) Which phantasies are more compelling than others
for the infant at a given moment is determined by the
interplay of the infant's constitution and actual experience. For Klein, the emphasis is clearly on the former:
"The strength of the ego—reflecting the state of fusion
between the two instincts—is, I believe, constitutionally
determined" (Klein, 1958, pp. 238–239).

Using the paradigm of codes analogous to the deep
structure of language, I would restate Klein's ideas in the
following way: The relative constitutional endowment of
life and death instincts[2] is the major determinant of which
code the infant will rely upon to interpret experience.
Experience interpreted in accord with the death instinct
will be attributed aggressive and dangerous meanings[3],

---

[2]It is beyond the scope of the present discussion to explore in any
detail the Kleinian conception of the life and death instincts. Very
schematically, the psychological correlates of the life instinct include
the loving, sexual, nurturing, attachment-seeking, and generative motivations, whereas the psychological correlates of the death instinct
include destructive, disintegrative, envious, and hostile motivations.
In the beginning, the infant experiences a sense of diffuse, internal
danger deriving from the death instinct. This sense of "nameless
dread" (Bion, 1962a), when defended against by means of splitting
and projective identification, results in the establishment of a persecutory object world split off from one's good objects. The nature of
the mental activity involved in this early stage of psychological organization (the paranoid-schizoid position) will be discussed in Chapter 3.

[3]Grotstein (1985), building upon the work of Bion, has proposed that
the death instinct be understood not as a caldron of destructive
impulses (Klein, 1952c), nor as the psychological correlate of entropy
(Freud, 1920), but as a system of inborn schemata serving to orient
the individual to potential danger. The infant is seen as constitutionally endowed with a set of preconceptions that allows him to interpret
experience in terms of possible danger of a prey–predator type. The

whereas experience organized in terms of the life instinct will be understood in terms of nurturing, loving meanings.

The role of actual experience with the mother is important, but secondary:

> To what extent the strength of the ego can be maintained and increased is in part affected by external factors, in particular, the mother's attitude towards the infant. However, even when the life instinct and the capacity for love predominate, destructive impulses are still deflected outwards and contribute to the creation of persecutory and dangerous objects which are re-introjected. (Klein, 1958, p. 239)

Actual experience may support an instinctual mode of organizing experience, but does not create the mode by which the experience is interpreted. For instance, persistent deprivation will lend emotional intensity to interpretations made in accord with the death instinct. Actual deprivation will confirm the infant's readiness to experience his object as dangerous. The sense of danger is not *created* by the deprivation; real danger simply confirms the infant's anticipation that such danger exists. Moreover, such anticipation of danger will not be entirely disconfirmed by the absence of actual danger. Interpreting experience along the lines of meaning that follow from the code connected with the death instinct will go on despite good experience: "Even the child who has a loving relation with his mother has also unconsciously a terror of

---

death instinct is conceived of as the origin of unconscious ego defenses as well as many of the primary autonomous ego functions which perform the function of seeking out and managing both internal and external danger.

being devoured, torn up, and destroyed by her" (Klein, 1963b, p. 277).

In Kleinian theory the instincts are conceived of as biologically determined organizations that utilize actual experience to link a "preconception" with its "realization" (Bion, 1962b). For example, the preconception of danger is linked with a facet of reality that can be experienced as dangerous. The preconception is not an idea but, rather, the potential for an idea. It is only in the linking of the preconception with the real that a conception (a thought) is generated.

Freud's Conception of "Inheritance of Knowledge"

I consider this understanding of the Kleinian concept of phylogenetically inherited "knowledge" (what Bion, [1962a] terms "preconception") to be an outgrowth of the second (chronologically) of Freud's two most fundamental contributions to psychology. The first of these contributions is his conception of the unconscious mind, the notion that one has thoughts, feelings, motivations, etc., of which one is unaware, but that nonetheless play a powerful role in determining the nature of one's observable thoughts, feelings, and behavior. The second of Freud's two monumental contributions was his theory of *sexual meanings*. I believe that the significance of this second cornerstone of psychoanalytic theory has to a considerable degree been lost sight of in recent years. Freud claimed not only that sexual desire is a terribly powerful human motivation, but also that it exists from birth. (This much of Freud's sexual theory is generally understood and appreciated, but I do not believe this to be the major significance of Freud's sexual theory.) Far more radical a proposal was Freud's notion that all human motivations, all human psychopathology, all human cultural achievements, all human behavior, can be understood in terms of *sexual meanings*.[4] From this perspective, the sexual instinct is not simply a striving, an impulse, a desire, but *the* vehicle by which human beings create meaning. In other words, Freud did not simply propose that the sexual instinct be thought of as generating sexual wishes and impulses. Of much wider significance is the implication that human beings interpret all perceptions in terms of sexual meanings, thereby *creating* experience. One makes sense of one's internal and external perceptions through the lens of the system of sexual meanings. To use still another metaphor, the sexual instinct is the Rosetta stone that allows the human being to translate raw sensory data into meaning-laden experience (see Greenberg and Mitchell, 1983, for a discussion of this idea from a different perspective).

Freud's theory of psychological development is built upon the notion of an inborn expectancy of particular constellations of meanings (including dangers specific to each phase of development) *where expectancy does not depend on actual experience*.[5] The universality of castration

---

[4]From the time Freud (1905) introduced the concept of instinct, he thought of the sexual instinct as accompanied by a second instinct (the ego instinct, and, as he came to maintain after 1920, the death instinct). As a result, instinct-derived psychological meanings were, for Freud, never exclusively sexual in nature. However, as can be seen, for example, in Freud's conceptions of the neuroses, his theory of instinct-derived meaning was most centrally a theory of sexual meaning.

[5]That Freud at times placed greater emphasis on inborn, phylogenetically determined schemata than on actual experience is unmistakable: "Whenever experiences fail to fit in with hereditary schema, they become remodelled in the imagination" (Freud, 1918, pp. 119).

anxiety, for example, is not simply the product of environmental factors; rather, experience serves as a trigger for
an inborn expectation of a specific form of bodily damage.
Further, the Oedipus complex as a whole is understood by
Freud as a universal mode of organizing and responding to
experience, and not simply as a feature of the family
environment to which the child responds. Here, again, one
is confronted by Freud's boldness: He not only suggested
that all human experience can be understood in terms of
sexual meanings, but proposed that the Oedipus complex
is a major principle by which these meanings (ultimately
sexual in nature) are organized. One can scarcely imagine
the enormity of the challenge Freud posed for himself in
attempting to discern a single system by which all human
meaning is created, a single lens through which all raw
sensory data are filtered, organized, and attributed meaning. And yet this is the puzzle for which Freud's theory of
sexuality and the Oedipus complex is the proposed solution.

   For Freud, phylogenetic inheritance is the basis for
the capacity of instinct to give rise to universal constellations of sexual meanings:

   Whence comes the need for these [universal sexual]
   phantasies and the material for them? There can be
   no doubt that their sources lie in the instincts; but it
   has still to be explained why the same phantasies with
   the same content are created on every occasion. I am
   prepared with an answer which I know will seem
   daring to you. I believe these *primal phantasies*, as I
   should like to call them, and no doubt a few others as
   well, are a phylogenetic endowment. In them, the
   individual reaches beyond his own experience into
   primaeval experience at points where his own expe-

rience has been too rudimentary. It seems to me quite possible that all the things that are told us today in analysis as phantasy—the seduction of children, the inflaming of sexual excitement by observing parental intercourse, the threat of castration (or rather castration itself)—were once real occurrences in the primaeval times of the human family, and that children in their phantasies are simply filling in the gaps in individual truth with prehistoric truth. I have repeatedly been led to suspect that the psychology of the neuroses has stored up in it more of the antiquities of human development than any other source. (Freud, 1916-17, pp. 370-371)

From this perspective, Klein has not introduced a radical departure from Freud's conceptualization of "inheritance" of knowledge; rather, she has expanded his notion of inherent readiness to organize experience in specific ways and extended it to preoedipal experience. In particular, she focused on the forms of preconception characterizing oral, anal, and early phallic levels of development. When Isaacs (1952) proposed that the infant's knowledge of the breast and his wish to tear it to bits be understood as inherent in the instincts, she was elaborating and extending to early phases of instinctual development, principles that are at the core of one of Freud's revolutionary contributions to psychology: the potential of instinct to serve as a Rosetta stone for man's attribution of meaning to experience.

For Klein, actual experience which varies considerably in different families, cultures, and eras serves to provide data to be organized in a highly predetermined way by the code inherent in the instincts. Using the analogy of the deep structure of language, a very wide range of phonemic data (the sound of actual spoken language) will provide sufficient "stimuli" for the infant to perceive and organize the sound units of language into a system that constitutes the syntactic and semantic structure of a particular language. Interaction with parenting figures, including exposure to spoken language, is essential, but not as a source of specific information about a method of constructing a grammar. Rather, actual experience triggers a sequence of inborn functions by which perceived speech sounds are organized.

In terms of the ethological analogy introduced earlier, the mother hen does not teach her chicks the details of the wing patterns of predators, nor does she teach them by example the adaptive fight and flight responses to the recognition of the predator. Instead, the mothering activities of the hen safeguard the chick's biologically determined maturational processes, which include complex, highly differentiated instinctual response patterns such as the ability to differentiate predator and non-predator, and to respond in a manner specific to each.

Bowlby's (1969) understanding of inborn attachment and separation behavior patterns is related to, although not identical to, the conception of psychological deep structure that I have outlined. Bowlby's focus is not on the psychological organization of meanings along particular lines but, rather, on the interplay of the environment and innate *behavioral systems*:

Attachment behavior . . . is held to have a biological function specific to itself. . . . Attachment behavior is regarded as what occurs when certain behavioral systems are activated. The behavioral systems themselves are believed to develop within the infant as a result of his interaction with his environment of

evolutionary adaptedness, and especially of his interaction with the principal figure in the environment,
namely his mother. (pp. 179–180)

Bowlby's theory is similar to the notion of psychological deep structure in that it focuses upon the unlearned,
"supra-individual" elements in attachment and separation
behavior. It differs from the psychoanalytic deep structure conception, however, in that it deals with *patterns of
behavior* rather than systems of generating and organizing
meaning.

*The Symbolic Form of
Early Phantasy Activity*

Thus far two aspects of the development of early mental
life have been put aside in order to focus on the process by
which "phylogenetic inheritance of knowledge" might
occur. Attention will now be focused on the way in which
early mental contents (primitive phantasies) are *experienced* by the infant. We are now asking: What, according
to Klein, is the form of symbolization utilized by the
infant (e.g., words, visual images, bodily sensations), and
what is the degree of subjectivity of which the infant is
capable?

I will address first the Kleinian notion of the form, as
opposed to the mode, of symbolization involved in early
phantasy activity. (The mode of symbolization involved in
the paranoid-schizoid position, i.e., symbolic equation,
will be discussed later.) One cannot help but become
skeptical about Kleinian early developmental theory, if
one understands the theory as portraying the infant as
engaged in symbolic mental activity comparable to adult

phantasy, differing only in the degree of primitivity of the contents. One frequently hears it said that the Kleinians imagine the infant capable of phantasy long before his symbolic (particularly verbal) capacities could possibly have developed to the point required for such activity. Such criticism is based on an incomplete understanding of the Kleinian conception of phantasy. The Kleinians do not limit the concept of phantasy to phantasies in the form of visual and verbal symbols: "At first, the whole weight of wish and phantasy is borne by sensation and affect" (Isaacs, 1952, p. 92).

If one is to understand Kleinian theory of early phantasy activity, one must always keep in mind that the Kleinians' written descriptions of early phantasies are necessarily in verbal terms and, therefore, are only indirectly related to an actual preverbal infantile phantasy. The infant does not think in verbal terms:

> The adult way of regarding the body and the mind as two separate sorts of experience can certainly not hold true of the infant's world. It is easier for adults to observe actual sucking than to remember or understand what the experience of sucking is to the infant, for whom there is no dichotomy of body and mind, but a single, undifferentiated experience of sucking and phantasying. Even those aspects of psychological experience which we later on distinguish as "sensation", "feeling", etc., cannot in the early days be distinguished and separated. Sensations, feelings, as such, emerge through development from the primary whole of experience, which is that of sucking—sensing—feeling—phantasying. This total experience becomes gradually differentiated into its various aspects of experience: bodily movements, sensations, imagin-

ings, knowings, and so on. (W. C. M. Scott, 1943, in Isaacs, 1952, pp. 92–93fn)

To begin to get a sense of the infant's phantasy experience, one must attempt the impossible in trying to imagine oneself outside the system of verbal symbols in which adults live and are trapped, and instead, to imagine oneself in a system of nonverbal, sensory experience (including kinesthetic and visceral experience). This act of imagination involves, in part, an attempt to think without words. Despite the extreme difficulty we have in imagining ourselves in the psychological state of the infant, there is nothing mystical about the idea of infantile phantasy. The discontinuity between the adult state and the infantile state can be understood to derive in part from the difference in form and mode of symbolic activity employed by infants from that used by children and adults. The fact that infantile phantasy is not directly observable poses no greater theoretical problem than the concept of the unconscious mind itself, which is by definition unobservable. As with the unconscious, only the derivatives of infantile phantasy are observable.

The Degree of Subjectivity and Mode of Symbolization in Early Phantasy Activity

In developing a sense of the nature of the Kleinian conception of early phantasy activity, we must at this point inquire into the way in which the Kleinians conceive of the place of the subject in relation to his signs and symbols in the process of re-presenting bodily experience in phantasy. In other words, one must attempt to understand how Klein conceived of the way in which the infant experiences himself in relation to his thoughts and sensations.

Klein is not explicit about the way in which she views the infant's experience of his early part–object relationships. The following is representative of Klein's discussions of the infant's feelings in relation to idealized and persecutory internal objects:

> It is characteristic of the emotions of the very young infant that they are of an extreme and powerful nature. The frustrating (bad) object is felt to be a terrifying persecutor, the good breast tends to turn into the "ideal" breast which should fulfill the greedy desire for unlimited, immediate, and everlasting gratification. Thus, feelings arise about a perfect and inexhaustible breast, always available, always gratifying. Another factor which makes for idealization of the good breast is the strength of the infant's persecutory fear, which creates the need to be protected from persecutors and therefore goes to increase the power of an all-gratifying object. The idealized breast forms the corollary of the persecuting breast; and insofar as idealization is derived from the need to be protected from persecuting objects, it is a method of defence against anxiety. (1952c, p. 64)

From this account and many others like it (see, for example, Klein, 1930), Klein leaves a fundamental question unaddressed: Is there a subjective self feeling frightened of bad objects and feeling protected by good ones; or is it simply a fact (experienced by no one in particular) that there is danger posed by bad objects and a corresponding need for protection provided by good objects? In the latter case (where things just happen), no subjectivity is involved; there is simply registration of sensation with an absence of a feeling of "I-ness," an absence of a sense of oneself as observer and creator of one's own thoughts, feelings, and perceptions. The language that Klein uses here is characteristic of her discussion of infantile phantasy in that she relies heavily on the passive voice to describe infantile experience: "the bad object is felt to be . . . ," "the good breast tends to turn into . . . ," "feelings arise . . . ," fears "create the need" for protection, the idealized object "is derived from the need to be protected." Only indirectly through this use of language is there indication that Klein conceives of early infantile experience as nonsubjective (that is, devoid of a sense of "I-ness").

The subsequent work of Kleinians (Bick [1968], Bion [1962a]), Meltzer [1975], Segal [1957], Tustin [1972], and others) has to a large degree moved toward a conception of early infantile experience as devoid of subjectivity. The infant's thoughts, feelings and perceptions are conceived of by these followers of Klein as constituting things in themselves, events that simply occur. The infant does not experience himself as having a point of view or perspective. There is no infant as thinker or interpreter of his experience. From an outsider's point of view, the infant interprets perceptions in, for example, a paranoid or a loving way. The infant, however, has no awareness of himself as interpreter of experience in the earliest phase of development (the paranoid-schizoid position). The self that does exist is the self as object, not the self as subject. (This state of being will be discussed in detail in Chapter 3.)

The Infant's Mental Capacities

At this point, the question again arises as to whether the Kleinians "really believe" that such complicated mental activity as that involved in the phantasy of tearing the breast to bits goes on in the first weeks and months of life.

Important questions remain, even given that infantile
phantasies as conceived by Klein are not verbally symbolized, do not presuppose the development of the symbolic
function further than the state of nonverbal symbolic
equation, and involve little, if any, subjectivity. How can
the Kleinians assume the presence of rather advanced
cognitive capacities in the first weeks of life? How can the
Kleinians assume that the capacity to differentiate outside
and inside, the capacity to represent the mother in her
absence, the capacity to differentiate self from nonself,
the capacity to differentiate the mother from other people,
etc., all exist in the first weeks of life when Piaget has
demonstrated that these capacities are not achieved until
significantly later in development?

I believe that Klein and her early circle (including
Isaacs, Rivière, Heimann, and Rosenfeld) did not have
available the data required to reply to these questions.
Isaacs (1952) invoked the concept of the continuity of
development in saying that, just as children understand
language before they can speak, phantasy activity requires
considerable development before evidence of phantasy is
seen in verbal productions and play activity.

I feel that a fuller consideration of the development
of mental capacities underlying phantasy activity can now
be made on the basis of the principles of development
emerging from the neonatal observational research of
Bower (1977), Brazelton (1981), Eimas (1975), Sander
(1975), Stern (1977), Trevarthan (1979), and others.
These data suggest that cognitive capacities do not develop
solely along a unitary chronological sequence of differen-
tiating and integrating structures. Few would question the
existence of the developmental sequence so elegantly demonstrated by Piaget (1936). Added to Piaget's understanding of cognitive development, however, is the notion of

the operation of capacities much earlier than expected where the operation of such capacities is necessary for the infant's participation in a life-sustaining, early form of relatedness to the mother, i.e., the mother–infant dialogue of the first days and weeks of life (see Grotstein, 1983; Stern, 1983).

Stern (1977) describes the infant's "innate predilection" for specific visual configurations making up the human face. The infant's capacity for shape and shading discriminations allows him to discern and select such configurations "without any previous specific learning experiences" (Stern, 1977, p. 36).

[The infant's] special interest [in the human face] is founded on a biological basis by virtue of the infant's innate bias for certain kinds and amounts of stimulation . . . the sharp angles provided by the corners of the eyes as well as the light-dark contrast of pupil and eye white (sclera) and of eyebrow and skin are especially fascinating to the infant. From the beginning, then, the infant is "designed" to find the human face fascinating. . . . (Stern, 1977, p. 37)

The infant very early on becomes able to differentiate the mother's face from other faces (Brazelton, 1981). However, the shape and shading discriminations involved in this cognitive task and the capacity for recall of these discriminations are not stabilized, nor are they generalized, and will not become a stable part of the observable, differentiated cognitive capacities demonstrable in Piagetian test situations until much later in development. (Piaget's [1954] stage of object permanence wherein the infant achieves the capacity to maintain a mental representation of an inanimate object in its absence does not occur until the last quarter of the first year of life.) Using this model of cognitive capacities developing along more than one timetable and *depending heavily on the specific emotional and interpersonal context,* one could entertain the possibility that the mental activity involved in the Kleinian conception of infantile phantasy may involve the more unstable and more context-limited cognitive operations that are out of synchrony with the development of the stable cognitive structures described by Piaget.

A second relevant trend emerging from the neonatal observational research of the last three decades is the idea that the infant uses more than one form of knowledge about objects. One form of knowledge seems to develop in a sequence of steps (each cognitive development building upon previous ones in a fashion that allows for increasingly complex mental operations); the other seems to be more intuitive in that it does not depend on a stepwise series of advances in mental functioning. For example, Bower (1971) has demonstrated that in the first weeks of life, infants have a sense of the continuity of the existence of the object over time and space. In one set of experiments, 20-day-old infants showed surprise when an object failed to reappear after a screen was removed that had been placed between the infant and the object. In another set of experiments, when an 8-week-old infant's view of a portion of the path of a moving object was occluded by a screen, the infant's eye and head movements anticipated the reappearance of the object at the other side of the screen before the object actually became visible in its new location.

It seems that even very young infants know that an object is there even after it has been hidden . . . The early age of the infant and the novelty of the test situation make it unlikely that such a response has been learned. (Bower, 1971, p. 35)

This early sense of continuity of matter over time and space could be thought of as an important part of the infant's "intuitive" sense of objects from birth. The consolidations of the sense of object permanence at 8 to 10 months and at 18 to 22 months reflect much more complex, more highly structured, and more stable cognitive achievements. Yet, this early anticipation of the absent object must be taken into account in assessing Klein's conception of the infant as capable of recalling the mother in her absence in the first weeks of life.

This early intuition about the nature of objects reflects the operation of psychological deep structures, inborn modes of organizing perception. To acknowledge that there are inborn modes of organizing experience is not to say that one has established that the infant is capable of the complexity of mental activity that Klein envisions or that the content of that mental activity is of the sort hypothesized by Klein.

The Role of the Environment

With this understanding of the Kleinian conception of instinct, phantasy, and preconception in mind, we can now consider Klein's idea about the infant's relationship to the environment. For Klein (1952c, 1957, 1958), the infant is at first a prisoner of his own state of mind which is not experienced as a state of mind. In the very beginning, the infant sees in the external world only what he expects to see on the basis of preconceptions (the organization of perception formed on the basis of inherited modes of organizing experience). These expectations are of two general types, reflecting the deep structures corresponding to the life and death instincts. For Klein, the death instinct generates more anxiety than the life instinct and initially exerts a far more powerful influence on the way the infant organizes experience. For Klein (1952a), the death instinct generates a sense of danger that is given specific shape as the infant organizes his perceptions (both internal bodily sensation and the perception of external objects) in accord with the mode of attribution of meaning inherent in that instinct. A second system of meaning is generated by the infant's organization of perception in accord with the life instinct. Imprisoned in his expectations, the infant is unable to learn from experience, because new experience is interpreted only in terms of these expectations. An analogous situation exists in the profoundly paranoid adult patient who experiences all new relationships in terms of his expectations of danger. Someone who is genuinely kind to the intensely paranoid patient is seen by the patient as fraudulent, manipulating the patient into a position of vulnerability. Similarly, the hypochondriacal patient experiences all bodily sensations in accord with his delusional sense of internal danger. Normal findings on physical and laboratory examinations are not the least bit reassuring, because these data are attributed meaning and denied meaning in accord with a self-fulfilling paranoid system.

To summarize, the infant, for Klein, initially creates his reality: "The child's earliest reality is wholly phantastic" (Klein, 1930, p. 238). In part this can be understood as a projection of the infant's internal world onto his external objects (Grotstein, 1980a). But even more basic than the notion of projection is the idea that the infant is incapable of doing anything but attributing meaning to experience on the basis of his inborn codes, the life and death instincts.

The question will now arise as to how the infant ever breaks out of the imprisonment of his preconceptions. How does the infant as conceived of by Klein ever become capable of learning from experience? One form of answer given by Kleinians is that, in combination with the biological maturation of the infant, good experiene *softens* the infant's conviction about the dangers in the world:

> When there is a predominance of good experience over bad experience, the ego acquires a belief in the prevalence of the ideal object over the persecutory objects and also of the predominance of its own life instinct over its own death instinct. (Segal, 1964, p. 37)

This is not an entirely satisfying answer, however; one wonders why the infant should trust good experience instead of dismissing it as a trick or deception.

The relative constitutional endowment of life and death instincts also figures largely in Kleinian thinking about the infant's capacity to emerge from this initially closed intrapsychic system. It is argued that if constitutional endowment of the life instinct is predominant over the death instinct, the projection of derivatives of the life instinct onto objects will allow for the creation of idealized good objects that serve to defend the ego against the persecutory objects. But this explanation does not explain the capacity of the infant to alter his relationship to bad objects other than by relying on idealized good objects to protect him against the danger. By analogy, the adult paranoid patient does not emerge from paranoia by developing a mental police force to protect him against danger.

A change in the *quality of the infant's experience of the bad object* is not explained by a quantitative shift in the balance of power between good and bad objects.

Although I do not find either of the aforementioned Kleinian explanations sufficient to account for the infant's acquisition of the capacity to learn from experience, I feel that implicit in one of Klein's concepts is a more penetrating understanding of this question. The concept to which I am referring is projective identification, which provides a way of understanding the way in which the infant is able to emerge from the closed system of his internal psychological world. Having superimposed his internal world on the external one, the infant is imprisoned until the mother allows herself to be used in a process through which a mother–infant entity is created that is neither infant nor mother, but a product of the two. Although Klein only implicitly conceived of the process of projective identification in this way,[6] I view it as that aspect of early development which allows the infant to move beyond himself (Ogden, 1979, 1981, 1982a).[7]

[6] In her two principal discussions of projective identification, Klein (1946, 1955) predominantly treated projective identification as an intrapsychic process utilized as a means of defending against anxiety generated by the death instinct. However, her examples and her use of language imply an interpersonal component of the process. She emphasizes that, in projective identification, unconscious contents are projected *"into"* (1946, p. 8), not *onto* the object. Bion (1962a) developed the idea of projective identification as a relationship of container and contained that serves not only as a defense, but as a form of communication in which two personality systems modify each another.

[7] The necessity for conceptualizing a process by which there is movement from a closed psychological system to an open one is not unique to the Kleinian theory of development. For Freud (1914), the infant must move from an intrapsychic state of "absolute narcissism"

Projective identification, as I understand it, allows the infant (more accurately, the mother–infant) to process experience in a way that differs qualitatively from anything that had been possible for the infant on his own. In projective identification, the projector induces a feeling state in another that corresponds to a state that the projector had been unable to experience for himself. The object is enlisted in playing a role in an externalized version of the projector's unconscious psychological state. When a "recipient" of a projective identification allows the induced state to reside within him without immediately attempting to rid himself of these feelings, the projector–recipient pair can experience that which had been projected in a manner unavailable to the projector alone.

Projective identification is not simply a process wherein the mother (as object of a projective identification) "metabolizes" experience for the infant (projector) and then returns it to him in a form that the infant can utilize. Although this is a common conception of projective identification, this understanding falls short in that it implies that the infant's receptivity remains unchanged throughout the process. Without a change in the infant's *way of experiencing* his perceptions, he would not be able to modify his expectations even if his projection had been modified by the mother and made available to him through

---

(p. 150) to a later stage of object relatedness and secondary narcissism. As with Klein, Freud never described the process by which the infant escapes his initially closed psychological system in which all psychological investment is in the self, other than to say that instinctual frustration forces reality upon the maturing infant and leads to the development of the reality principle. The impetus for the development of an open psychological system is accounted for in this way, but the psychological and interpersonal processes that mediate this change remain unspecified.

her empathic caregiving. I believe that a form of psychological activity qualitatively different from the "metabolizing" or "processing" conception of the role of the mother in projective identification is involved in the infant's initial movement out of the closed system of his internal world. In projective identification, a potential for a certain quality of experience is generated by the mother–infant entity. Lacan (1956b) refers to the new psychological entity created by mother and infant (or patient and analyst) as "the Other." The mother–infant of successful projective identification is an entity greater than either individual alone and is capable of generating a quality of being that neither individual alone could have generated.

I feel that the terms *processing* and *metabolizing* are misleading when referring to the psychological activity of the object of a projective identification; these terms refer to a psychological activity that the recipient alone could engage in, independently of the projector. Bion's (1962a) concept of the container and the contained more accurately represents the situation. Containment involves not only an alteration of that which has been projected, but also an alteration of the projector in the process of creating the type of emotional linkage that is involved in projective identification.

I believe that Donald Winnicott's work on primary maternal preoccupation (1956), the stage of illusion (1951), and potential space (1971) can be understood as a development of the notion of projective identification as a form of simultaneous oneness and twoness (unity and separateness of mother and infant) that in turn creates a potential for a form of experience that is more generative than the sum of the individual psychological states contributing to it. (See Chapters 7 and 8 for further discussion of the relationship of the concept of projective identification to Winnicott's concept of potential space.)

With this understanding of projective identification in mind, we can say that Kleinian thinking includes an implicit conception of the importance of the environment, although Klein herself may not have fully recognized this implication of the concept of projective identification. Without the mother's serving as container for the infant's projective identifications, the infant would be doomed to an autistic or psychotic existence. Bion (1959, 1962a) refers to the mother's inability or unwillingness to accept the infant's projective identification as an "attack on linkage." This behavior is then internalized by the infant in the form of self-directed attacks on efforts to link thoughts and to generate emotional ties (linkages) to other people. This process, according to Bion (1959), is an essential factor in the etiology of schizophrenia and other severe emotional disturbances.

From the perspective of the understanding of projective identification that I have outlined, the conception of early development proposed by Klein need not undervalue the environment, the real mother, since the mother serves as a key partner in the shared psychological process constituting projective identification. This conception of the mother–infant of projective identification as the basic psychological unit of earliest development provides what I believe to be a far more satisfactory explanation than those explicitly offered by Klein for the infant's capacity to develop beyond the confines of his inherited system of preconceptions.

Concluding Comments

Melanie Klein has enriched psychoanalytic theory through her attempts to delineate the nature of very early mental activity. The intense and often heated debate over

Kleinian developmental theory has centered almost exclusively on the dating of the appearance of mental activity,
i.e., phantasy; the degree of specificity of early phantasy
activity; the predominantly aggressive and persecutory
content attributed to these phantasies; and the divergence
of such a conception from a Piagetian conception of the
formation of cognitive capacities.

The circumscribed focus of this debate has obscured
a number of important features of the Kleinian contribution. First, in any developmental theory, the proposed
sequence and interrelationship of developmental phases is
of far greater significance than a precise dating of events.
One does Kleinian theory a disservice by dismissing it on
the basis of an implausible chronology before considering
the possible value of its revised conception of levels of
early psychological organization.[8]

Second, there is a tendency in discussing Klein to
view her ideas as pronouncements to be accepted or rejected, rather than hypotheses to be modified in accord
with subsequent theoretical advances and new clinical and
observational data.

When Kleinian theory is taken as a set of hypotheses
to be modified, extended, or in part discarded, one generates a frame of mind in which it becomes possible to build
upon what is implicit in the theory (even when Kleinians
themselves seem unaware of a particular potential of their
ideas). For example, the Kleinian notion that knowledge
of objects is inherent in the aim of the instinct lends itself

[8]I fully concur with Winnicott's (1954) comments distinguishing the
timetable from specific conceptual contents within Klein's developmental theory: "If I find an analyst claiming too much for the
depressive position in the development that belongs to the first six
months of life, I feel inclined to make the comment: what a pity to
spoil a valuable concept by making it difficult to believe in" (p. 163).

to being developed into a conception of psychological deep structure analogous to Chomsky's notion of linguistic deep structure. This is a necessary component of any psychoanalytic developmental theory and does not simply represent an effort to make plausible a Kleinian conception of phylogenetic inheritance. In addition, the idea of projective identification has been developed by Bion and others into a concept that bridges the intrapsychic and the interpersonal despite the fact that Klein herself only minimally developed this aspect of her thinking.

Third, focusing on the more apparent difficulties in Kleinian theory (e.g., the early developmental timetable) obscures other significant limitations of Kleinian thinking. For example, one of the most limiting features of Klein's developmental theory is her conception of the infant as an independent psychological entity capable of wishes and defenses that are projected onto and into objects that constitute independent psychological systems. Not only did Klein undervalue the role of the environment, but she seems to have had little conception of the mother–infant as the basic psychological unit undergoing development in the beginning. Paradoxically, I feel that Klein's concept of projective identification can be utilized as the basis for a conception of the creation of the mother–infant psychological unit as Bion has done in his conception of the container and the contained and as Winnicott has done in his conception of an early stage of illusion and in his concept of potential space.

3

The Paranoid-Schizoid Position: Self as Object

The affirmation, "I live" is only conditionally correct, it expresses only a small and superficial part of the principle, "Man is lived by the It."

—*George Groddeck*

Melanie Klein's view of psychological development can be viewed as a biphasic progression from the biological to the impersonal-psychological, and from the impersonal-psychological to the subjective. The first of these developmental advances involves a transformation of the infant as a purely biological entity into the infant as a psychological entity. For Klein, this transformation is mediated by what I have termed *psychological deep structures* associated with the life and death instincts. Phantasy is a reflection of the operation of these psychological deep structures, just as speech is the "product of" linguistic deep structures. For

Klein, the shift from the biological to the psychological constitutes the entry of the infant into the paranoid-schizoid position. As will be discussed, the paranoid-schizoid position is a phase of development wherein the self exists predominantly as object. This is a developmental phase of "it-ness," wherein the infant is lived by his experience. Thoughts and feelings happen to the infant rather than being thought or felt by the infant.

The transition from the paranoid-schizoid position to the depressive position, wherein a subjective "I" emerges, is made possible by the biological maturation of the infant and is mediated by the psychological-interpersonal process of projective identification. The depressive position constitutes a more complex psychological organization, wherein a new realm of experience, a new state of being,[1] is generated.

I believe that Klein's concepts of the paranoid-schizoid and depressive positions represent important contributions to a psychoanalytic understanding of basic psychological states of being that are developed in infancy and persist throughout life. Unfortunately, because these ideas have been treated as inseparable from the body of Kleinian theory, an understanding of these concepts has

---

[1]When I speak of a *state of being*, I have in mind that aspect of psychological experience having to do with what it feels like to be alive. The quality of a given state of being is a reflection of the degree of subjectivity (the experience of "I-ness") that has been achieved; the psychological location of this subjectivity in relation to the individual's thoughts, his mind, his body, the not-I; the experience of the psychological space in which one thinks one's thoughts, lives in one's body, dreams one's dreams; the sense of the place of one's experience in relation to one's past and one's future; the degree of differentiation of one's self, one's symbols, and the symbolized.

not been integrated into the dialogue that constitutes American psychoanalytic thinking.

In thinking about Klein's proposal that the paranoid-schizoid position represents a universal, normative developmental phase dominated by a defensive response to the death instinct, one should also consider the possibility that the paranoid-schizoid position represents a breakdown phenomenon resulting from the premature disruption of primitive connectedness of mother and infant. When the paranoid-schizoid position is viewed from the latter perspective, i. e., as the result of the breakdown of the maternal "holding environment" (Winnicott, 1960b), the state of fearfulness associated with the paranoid-schizoid position need not be understood as a response to the death instinct but, rather, as a response to the disruption of the primitive interpersonal bond of mother and infant.

Splitting

In the previous chapter, I discussed the Kleinian conception of the manner in which early development is shaped by the infant's instinctual endowment. I suggested that the structuring of experience provided by the instincts can be thought of as the manifestation of psychological deep structure analogous to Chomsky's (1957, 1968) concept of linguistic deep structure. The deep structures associated with the life and death instincts lead the infant to organize experience in terms of anticipated dangers (reflecting the operation of the death instinct [see Grotstein, 1985]) and anticipated object attachments (reflecting the operation of the life instinct).

For Klein, the first psychological task of the infant is the management of danger generated by the death instinct.

Klein (1952c) conceived of this danger as being experienced by the infant as a threat of internal destructiveness[2] that must somehow be managed. The most basic
mode of management of danger is that of separating the
endangering from the endangered. Logic and volition are
no more involved in this pattern of defense than they are
in the neurologic reflexes of the newborn infant (e.g., the
sucking and grasping reflexes). The attempt to attain
safety by separating the endangered from the endangering
is an inherited mode of response to danger—it is a biological phenomenon with psychological manifestations.

Although Klein did not use ethological analogies, I
would see splitting as analogous to the chick's unlearned
response to the perception of the hawk's wing pattern. The
chick's reaction is to flee and not to attack the hawk
(unless cornered), i.e., to separate itself from the danger
(Lorenz, 1937; Tinbergen, 1957). I understand splitting to
be a similarly biologically determined mode of managing
danger. (The process of splitting can be understood in this
way, whether or not one views, as Klein did, the derivatives of the death instinct as the ultimate source of
danger.) In the course of development, this biologically
determined mode of managing danger is elaborated psychologically. Each of the primitive psychological defenses
can be understood as constructions based upon the mode
of managing danger seen in splitting, i.e., built upon the
biologically determined effort to create safety by distanc-

[2]The instinctual code associated with the death instinct serves to
organize the sense of danger into object-related narratives, (e.g., prey-
predator phantasies [see Grotstein, 1985]). Bion (1962a) described
the pathological degeneration of object-related phantasies of danger
into a sense of "nameless dread" that occurs when the mother is
unwilling or unable to process the infant's projective identifications.

ing the endangered from the endangering. Projection, for example, can be understood as an effort in phantasy to remove an internal danger by locating the danger outside of oneself, i.e., separating oneself from it as if it were located in another. Introjection is used to separate a valued external object from an endangering one, by locating one or the other of these external objects within oneself and thereby protecting the valued object. Denial separates oneself from the dangerous object by emotionally treating the object as if it had been annihilated.

In the early stage of development that is under discussion, these defensive activities are reactions as opposed to responses. Biological automaticity has been transformed into psychological automaticity. Although Klein did not explicitly address the question of subjectivity, it seems implicit in Klein's clinical and theoretical accounts that in the paranoid-schizoid position, there is no interpreting subject mediating between perception of danger and response to it. The fact that this is a psychology without a subject is the basic paradox of the paranoid-schizoid position. Psychological experience of the type being described exists in itself, but not for a self. Further, it must be kept in mind that for patients operating in a predominantly paranoid-schizoid mode, thoughts and feelings are palpable objects and forces that appear, disappear, contaminate, transform, destroy, rescue, etc. For example, a patient operating in a paranoid-schizoid mode may shake his head to get rid of tormenting feelings, may literally put his thoughts into a letter and send the letter to the person who should hold these thoughts, or may request x-rays in order to be able to see the thing inside of him that is driving him crazy (see Ogden, 1979, 1981, 1982b for clinical examples of such reification and transposition of mental phenomena).

Projective identification develops as a psychological-interpersonal elaboration of the process of splitting. In the beginning, the infant is confronted with raw sensory data that must be attributed meaning before this stimulation can be transformed into experience. Sensory data, before they are attributed meaning (transformed into what Bion [1962a] calls "alpha elements"), are simply things-in-themselves (which Bion refers to as "beta elements"). For example, the infant's low blood sugar level is physiologically registered, but this event does not yet constitute the experience of hunger, which involves an attribution of meaning to sensory data. Bion (1962a, 1962b) believes that the creation of meaning is initially an interpersonal process mediated by an early form of projective identification. In this psychological-interpersonal process, the infant projects beta elements (sensory data prior to their transformation into personally meaningful experience) into the mother, who, through her containment of the projective identification, transforms the infant's things-in-themselves into meaningful experience (e.g., hunger). The infant then reinternalizes the experience in a form that he can use to generate his own thoughts and feelings. Through this early form of projective identification, experience is created interpersonally from which the infant is able to learn.[3]

More mature forms of projective identification are developed once the infant, child, or adult has developed the capacity to generate meanings for himself. Under such circumstances, projective identification involves a fantasy

[3]It seems to me that, given the framework Bion is proposing, the notion that beta elements are projected by the infant into the mother presupposes that these elements have acquired some degree of meaning. Otherwise, it would be difficult to imagine why they would be noticed or singled out for "ejection."

of expelling these split-off internal contents and of taking control of another person from within (Klein, 1946, 1955). Associated with this fantasy is an actual interpersonal interaction in which pressure is exerted on the other person to experience himself and behave in a manner congruent with the projector's unconscious phantasy (Bion, 1959). The recipient who successfully manages the feelings engendered in him makes available to the projector (through the interaction) a modified, more integrable version of the set of meanings that had been previously impossible to manage (Langs, 1976; Malin and Grotstein, 1966; Ogden, 1979).[4]

Having discussed various defensive uses of splitting (including splitting as an aspect of projective identification), it must be emphasized that splitting is not simply a defense; it is even more basically a mode of organizing experience. This form of mental operation is used in the beginning to create order out of the chaos of the infant's earliest experience on the basis of categories inherent in his instinctual deep structure. Splitting is a binominal ordering of experience, i.e., a dividing of experience into categories of pleasure and unpleasure, danger and safety, hunger and satiation, love and hate, me and not-me, and so on.

In the paranoid-schizoid position an interpreting subject with a continuous personal history maintained

---

[4]I believe that a revision of this understanding of projective identification is required. As was alluded to in Chapter 2, I feel that projective identification must be understood in terms of the creation of a new psychological unit (the mother–infant or projector–recipient), the formation of which accounts for the ability of the projector to move beyond his previous mode of organizing experience, i.e., to move beyond himself. Further discussion of this form of mental activity will be presented in Chapters 7 and 8.

through conscious and unconscious memory has not yet developed. As a result, in splitting, each event exists in itself, but not for a self existing over time or in relation to anything but itself. As will be discussed, the process of repression which is developed in the depressive position involves the preservation of a whole object even in its exile from awareness. Splitting is a boundary-creating mode of thought and therefore a part of an order-generating (not yet a personal meaning-generating) process.

Presubjective Experience

To the point in development discussed thus far, for Klein, there is not yet a person interpreting his experience. There is not yet an "I." The paranoid-schizoid position is the realm of "the it," even though it is not exclusively the realm of the id (i.e., instinctual pressures). In other words, the early ego (the adaptive organizing component of personality) is also impersonal in that it is practically devoid of subjectivity, a sense of "I-ness." The infant, when faced with the threat of danger generated by the processing (not yet an interpreting) of experience in accord with the death instinct, utilizes splitting. Splitting is an attempt at achieving safety by putting distance between the endangering and the endangered aspects of oneself and one's objects.

Objects are valuable, but there is not yet an "I" to love them or value them. The self that exists is the self as object, as opposed to the subjective self. The subjective self could be thought of as represented by the self-reflective awareness of "I am" in the sentence "I am being attacked." The "I am" is a condensation of "I am aware that I experience myself as . . ." The self in the paranoid-schizoid position is the self as object, not the self as

creator and interpreter of one's thoughts, feelings, perceptions, and the like. The self as object corresponds to an
unspoken, nonreflective self in the sentence "It's hot" (as
opposed to "I am aware that it feels hot to me") or "He's
dangerous" (as opposed to "I am aware that I experience
him as dangerous").[5]

On several occasions, I have worked with, or have
had presented to me in supervision, patients who did not
use personal pronouns in their speech and used very few
active verb forms. For example, a hospitalized, acutely
psychotic schizophrenic patient, having been hit by
another patient, said, "In kitchen . . . fuck . . . face smash
. . . crack . . . son of a bitch." This use of language
captures some of the state of being of the paranoid-schizoid position in which things simply happen. In work with a
borderline patient, a similar but less extreme omission of
personal pronouns occurred: "Went to school today . . .
no luck . . . teacher's a prick . . . hate him." As this went
on session after session, I was increasingly struck by the
way in which the patient did not experience himself as an
active personal agent but, rather, as an object to whom life
events occured.

Faulkner has captured the experience of the nonreflective self in the character of the "idiot" in *The Sound*

---

[5]This conception of a nonreflective state overlaps to a degree with
Sartre's (1943) notion of *being-in-itself*, a form of being that simply is
what it is: "Being-in-itself has no *within* which is opposed to a *without*
and which is analogous to a judgment, a law, a consciousness of itself.
The in-itself has nothing secret; it is a solid. In a sense we can
designate it as a synthesis. But it is the most indissoluble of all: the
synthesis of itself with itself" (p. lxvi). This aspect of being is absolutely undifferentiated from itself and is therefore a far more extreme
form of objectivity (nonreflectiveness) than that associated with the
paranoid-schizoid position.

and the Fury: "Ben ceased whimpering. He watched the spoon as it rose to his mouth. It was as if even eagerness were muscle-bound in him too, and hunger itself inarticulate, not knowing it is hunger."

Split Object Relations

The infant, in addition to dividing his objects into categories that help to separate the endangering and the endangered, also divides his perception of himself for the same purpose. The object, according to Klein (1946), is never split without a corresponding split of the ego. Facets of object-related experience are isolated from one another. The loving self (as object) stands in relation to the loving object, and is set apart from the hating self (as object) and the hating object. In splitting, one form of relationship between self and object is split from other experiences of oneself in relation to the other. It is more accurate to say that the infant generates part-object relationships than it is to say he creates part-objects, because there is always a self (as object) in the experience of oneself in relation to the other.

The successful feeding experience (or any other experience involving a successful "fitting together" of mother and infant) generates a feeling of a contented, loved self in relation to a loving object. A frustrating feed, on the other hand, generates the sense of a hating self in relation to a dissatisfying, hurtful object. (For Klein [1952b], the infant's projections determine to a very great extent whether a given feed is experienced as loving or hurtful.) *These loving and hurtful facets of experience (part-object relationships) are isolated from one another because it is too dangerous for the primitively organized infant to love the object he hates, and hate the object he loves, and upon whom the infant is absolutely dependent.* Instead, the infant uses omnipotent thinking, projection, introjection, denial, idealization, and projective identification to rearrange his internal object world in an effort to separate endangered aspects of self and object from their endangering aspects. The hating self and its relation to a hating object is split off from the loving self in relation to a loving object. When, for example, a hating object is felt to pose an internal danger to a loving aspect of self, the infant in phantasy ejects the endangered aspect of self into an external object, in order to create some distance between the dangerous object and the self. In projective identification there is an interpersonal component of the process that accompanies the projective phantasy. The infant as projector experiences himself as having been depleted of lovable parts of himself and may then feel all the more dependent on the object who is felt to contain all that is good (Klein, 1946).

Loving aspects of self, having previously been projected outward in order to safeguard them from internal danger, may later be felt to be endangered by a hating external object. Internalization of either the hating external object or the loved one will temporarily secure a modicum of safety. Inevitably, new dangers (actual and phantasied) come about and require new arrangements of parts of self and part-objects. Associated with the belief in the value of separating the endangering from the endangered are specific beliefs about how this safety is achieved, for example, the phantasy that one can better control an object that is within oneself, and the phantasy that an ejected object has been banished and will never return.

This, then, is the phenomenology and mode of operation of the paranoid-schizoid position. The paranoid-schizoid position is in ascendancy, according to Klein (1948), in the first three months of life, and is followed in the fourth to seventh months by the depressive position. The term *position* is used to refer to a level of psychological organization with its characteristic form of object related-ness, form of symbolization, modes of defense, type of anxiety, maturity of ego and superego functioning, etc. These "positions" are not passed through but, rather, continue throughout life as co-existing modes of organiz-ing and processing experience (Klein, 1952a; Bion, 1950, 1963), each generating a distinctive quality of being. (The relationship between the paranoid-schizoid and the depres-sive positions will be discussed in the next chapter.)

The paranoid-schizoid position is "schizoid" because in this phase, the infant relies heavily upon splitting of self and object as a defense and mode of organizing expe-rience; it is "paranoid" because the infant relies on pro-jective phantasies and projective identification in an effort to defend himself against object-related dangers, which, according to Klein (1948), represent a system of meanings derived from the death instinct. The leading anxiety of the paranoid-schizoid position is the fear of annihilation of oneself and one's valued objects. This does not mean that all infants are paranoid schizophrenics. On the contrary, it is an inability to adequately employ splitting that, among other conditions, can lead to severe psychopathology, in-cluding schizophrenia.

Failure of Splitting

The plight of a psychotic adolescent can be understood in terms of the patient's inability to use splitting effectively:

H., a 14-year-old boy who was hospitalized on a long-term analytically oriented ward, where I saw him in daily psychotherapy, was tortured by self-accusatory thoughts during virtually every waking moment and frequently in his dreams. Each time he touched an object he became frightened that he would be accused of attempting to steal it. Every woman he looked at triggered fears that he would be accused of intending to rape her or of having obscene thoughts about her. Each time he saw a man, he became frightened that he would be accused of being a homosexual, or that he would call the man a queer, and that the man would then retaliate.

Frequently, in the course of a day, the patient's internal psychological barrage would become so intense that he would scream in pain. In conscious and unconscious phantasy he "dumped" his internal state (his "sick brain") into me. He communicated his plight to me by bombarding me in the way he felt bombarded. The sessions were filled with an endless stream of threats, name-calling, and pounding of my office furniture, walls, and doors that at times reached almost deafening proportions. H. was careful not to do any "real damage." When this became a danger, he redoubled his assaults on himself. He told me on many occasions that he would give anything for just five seconds of peace. Although he never once acknowledged valuing me or the therapy, he arrived a half-hour early to each meeting "in order to shit on" me by relentlessly ringing the waiting room buzzer.

Everything that this patient thought and felt (in phantasy) became contaminated. In the transference he could not love me or value me without fearing that it would be tainted love, e.g., homosexual, incestuous, greedy, or damaging. The patient's powerful sense that every facet of emotional life is contaminated or about to be contaminated, is the hallmark of a primitive inadequacy of splitting. From H.'s (unconscious) point of view, he loved hatefully and hated lovingly, and therefore was terrified of doing either.

The infant must be able to split in order to feed safely without the intrusion of the anxiety that he is harming his mother, and without the anxiety that she will harm him. It is necessary for an infant to feel that the mother who is taking care of him is fully loving and has no connection whatever with the mother who "hurts" him by making him wait. The anxiety arising from the thought that the nurturing mother and the frustrating mother are one and the same would rob the infant of the security that he needs in order to feed safely. Similarly, the ability to desire safely would be lost if the infant, while feeding, experienced himself as the same infant who angrily wished to control and to subjugate the breast/mother in her absence. While feeding, the infant must experience himself as loving in an uncomplicated, uncontaminated way in order to be able to feel that he can want without damaging.

Splitting not only safeguards the infant's need to give and receive love; it also safeguards his need to hate. If the object of the infant's hate is contaminated with facets of the loved object, the infant will not be able to hate it safely. (The assumption that the infant has a need to hate is not dependent upon the Kleinian assumption of the presence of powerful, constitutionally determined destructive wishes. For instance, one could postulate, as did Winnicott [1947, 1957] and Fairbairn [1944], that hate arises from excessively frustrated need and that it is essential for normal development that the infant, child, or adult be able to experience this feeling without being frightened by it.)

Ms. K., a 23-year-old anorectic/bulimic patient being treated in intensive individual therapy, evidenced a compulsive need to vomit out hated and hating internal contents (food in her stomach that she feared would make her fat, and that was making her stomach painfully bloated).

She would not permit herself to move from the tenement in which she was living into a "decent apartment," which she could have afforded easily. The patient felt unable to move because she did not want to eat and vomit in a "nice place," nor did she want to or feel able to give up "bingeing" and vomiting. The therapist understood the patient's refusal/inability to move from her present apartment as a wish to retain her method of hating in an uncontaminated way. Moving into the new apartment would have entailed an act of love (of herself) that she did not want contaminated by the eating binges followed by vomiting (a symbolic act of violent hatred of her mother and herself).

Both loving and hating, after all, are necessary parts of the spectrum of human emotion and the patient could not give up hating in order to love, even if taking care of herself by moving out of the tenement seemed to her like the "sane thing to do." On the other hand, she did not want to give up loving (by not moving into an adequate apartment) in order to hate (which she equated with bingeing and vomiting), and as a result felt unable to make a decision.

The following clinical material is taken from an intensive psychotherapy of an 18-year-old woman with anorexia nervosa.

Over a period of almost a year, Ms. S. starved herself almost to death because her mother's food (which she generalized to include all food) was "too rich." This patient professed deep love for her mother and was unable to think of a single thing about her mother that she did not like and admire. Not only was her mother's food too rich, it was also at times felt to be "too good to eat"; in fact, the patient did not even like to see her mother's food being cooked because it was too good to cook. Eventually, in the course of therapy, one of the patient's central underlying conflicts was clarified: her mother was "too good to hate." (This was not a matter of failure of repression in relation to an ambivalently loved mother; this patient was unable to utilize effectively even the more primitive defense of splitting in relation to a mother experienced as a collection of part-objects.)

Unable to split off the hated aspect of her mother, the patient subsumed this aspect in the good aspect of the mother, where the hated aspect was disguised as "too much of a good thing." This is quite the opposite of ambivalence; it is an inability to separate the hated and the loved, followed by a disguising of the hated as the loved. The following dual dilemma resulted: 1. an inability to hate (very few patients that I have seen have been less able to directly experience a feeling of anger), and 2. an inability to love (the patient's inability to eat and in that way symbolically provide love or accept love for herself).

In summary, splitting allows the infant to feed safely and to love, and to desire and hate safely, without developing overwhelming anxiety that he is being destroyed by, or destroying that which he loves.

Failure of Integration

Splitting, although most basically a mode of organizing experience, comes to serve a defensive function. (This situation is analogous to that of the development of language itself: although language is fundamentally a medium for thinking and communicating, it secondarily acquires defensive functions.) As has been discussed, splitting as an early defense serves primarily to regulate, by mutual isolation, the relationship of loving and hating facets of experience. An inability to diminish one's reliance upon splitting reflects excessive anxiety about the dangers involved in the interpenetration of different feeling states, particularly love and hate. Splitting processes, fueled by anxiety of this type, become rigid and unchanging.

The following clinical vignette illustrates some of the behavioral and experiential correlates of continued reliance upon splitting as a defense.

Ms. N., a patient being seen in intensive psychotherapy, carried on a cluster of simultaneous but completely separate relationships that included a comforting relationship with her husband, whom she "mothered" and by whom she was mothered, and a highly sensual relationship with an older man. The patient's husband knew nothing of the older man, and the other man knew almost nothing about the husband. Neither man was told about the therapist, and the therapist was told only highly edited data

about the other two men. The patient became aware
that when she was with one of these three men, it was
almost as if the other two men did not exist. Much
more distressing than the discontinuity of her object
world was the realization that the person whom she
felt herself to be when with her husband barely
existed when she was with the older man. Frequently,
while at home, Ms. N. would experience a panicky
feeling of loss that would send her running back to
the other man. This was done not simply to reclaim
the lost object, but, perhaps even more important,
to reclaim a missing part of herself. When with the
older man, she would become distraught about the
other missing part of herself and would then anx-
iously return to her husband.

The patient felt that the relationship with the
therapist held the potential to bring her "together in
one place." Throughout this phase of the therapy,
however, the patient also experienced the therapist as
dangerous because she felt he might interfere with
her delicate system by demanding that she give up the
affair, the marriage, or the therapy. Ms. N. felt that
having to make such a choice would literally drive
her crazy. The patient was able to understand the
ways in which this fear was similar to childhood fears
that she would have to choose between her feuding
parents, between her parents and her sister, between
herself as her parents saw her and herself as she
viewed herself.

Ms. N. used splitting to generate a group of part-
object relationships, each with its own sense of self
and set of conscious and unconscious object-related
phantasies. Splitting was utilized in an effort not to
have to make choices between these facets of expe-

rience because to choose one would be in effect to annihilate the other aspects of herself. Ms. N. used lying (unnecessary elaborations of the truth to make a story better than it was), promiscuity, and petty theft in an attempt to feel more alive and present. Splitting had not only resulted in compartmentalization of her life, it had robbed each sector of vitality, since she could never feel fully present in any given situation or relationship. This is the experiential referent for the idea that whenever the object is split there is a corresponding splitting of the ego. Part of the experience of splitting of the ego is a feeling that part of oneself is missing since any given part-object relationship of necessity reflects only one isolated aspect of oneself.

Early Stages of Integration

Paradoxically, the achievement of adequate splitting is the necessary groundwork for the eventual integration of part-objects and parts of self into whole objects and a continuous sense of self. The reason for this is that it is only when one has achieved relative freedom from the anxiety that loving experience is, or is about to be, contaminated by hating experience, and vice versa, that one may dare to bring these different facets of experience into closer relation with each other.

A borderline patient, after many years of therapy, conveyed the experiential level of the achievement of adequate splitting in the following way: she said that, until that point, her fantasies and dreams had frequently contained lines or forms that went off endlessly in two directions. Now, for the first time, her fantasies contained lines

that had two ends. This change represented an enhance-
ment of the patient's capacity for adequate splitting: each
end of a line is tangibly different from its opposite end.
Each is distinctly itself and not the other. Each cannot be
mixed up with, confused with, or contaminated by the
other.

The following is an example of the earliest stages of
integration of an extreme form of pathologically split object relations.

A 46-year-old, chronically psychotic paranoid schizophrenic was treated over a period of many years in a
clinic, where he bullied and intimidated the staff as
well as the other patients. At times he had menac-
ingly pinned staff members against the wall and had
thrown furniture around the waiting room. The patient, Mr. E., unconsciously relied upon hostile part-
object relatedness as a defense against affectionate
relatedness, since the latter feelings were invariably
connected with a terrifying sense of physically becoming the other person. He could feel his chin
becoming the other person's chin. From there, he
experienced the rest of his face, and then his entire
body, becoming that of the other person. The therapist commented that the patient's suspiciousness,
guardedness, and fearfulness all served to make it feel
less likely that this physical tranformation would take
place.

In a session in this period of the therapy, Mr. E.
reported a strange experience. He had spoken with a
man outside of his building whom he had known for
many years who "favored" him. (The word *favored*
has a double meaning, particularly in the South,
where the patient grew up, of *physically resembling*
and of *acting kindly toward*. For this patient, the two

meanings were unconsciously inseparable.) Mr. E. was extremely disturbed by the fact that he saw in the man's face "an ugly beauty," something he had never encountered before. The patient, in a way that reflected an uncharacteristic groundedness and presence, asked the therapist if he knew what the patient was talking about, and if he had ever seen such a thing himself. Mr. E.'s calm, unthreatening, and yet persistent asking of the therapist if he knew of such a feeling was understood by the therapist as the patient's way of asking the therapist what his response would be to this new mixture (initial integration) of hostile and affectionate transference feelings (displaced onto the man encountered on the street).

Splitting as Discontinuity of History

In the paranoid-schizoid position, the predominant mode of symbolization ("symbolic equation," Segal, 1957) is one in which the symbol and the symbolized are emotionally indistinguishable since there is no interpreting self to mediate between symbol and symbolized. There is no sense that one attributes meaning to one's perception; events are what they are, and interpretation and perception are treated as identical processes. Sensory experience is unmediated[6] by an interpreting subject.

[6]Lacan's (1949-1960) conception of the realm of the imaginary (prior to the entry into the symbolic order) and Hegel's (1807) conception of the nature of nondialectical or predialectical "unselfconscious," "unself-aware" experience also involve conceptions of unmediated (immediate) sensory experience. For Lacan, it is the system of linguistic symbols that allows one to mediate between oneself and one's lived sensory experience. For Hegel, this is achieved through the mediation of work (man's productions) that is done for purposes other than that required for man's survival as an animal.

Within this state of mind, splitting generates a distinct quality of experience (state of being) quite different from that which develops later. The mental operation of splitting creates a state of mind in which there is "no in-between." A plane has two faces and two faces only; an observer can never see both sides at once. (This state stands in contrast to a situation where different facets of experience create and negate one another, always standing in relation to the other in the mind of the observer.) In the paranoid-schizoid position, there is no psychological vantage point from which more than one emotional plane can be taken in.

When a borderline patient feels angry at and disappointed by the therapist, he feels that he has now discovered the truth. The therapist is unreliable, and the patient should have known it all along. What had previously been seen by the patient as evidence of the therapist's trustworthiness, now is seen to have been an act of deception, a mask, a cover-up for what has become apparent. The truth is now out, and the patient will not deceive himself or be caught off guard again. *History is instantaneously rewritten.* The therapist is not the person the patient thought he was; he is now discovered to be someone new. Each time I have arrived at this juncture in a therapy, I have been freshly stunned by the coldness of the patient's renunciation of shared experience. There is an assault on the emotional history of the object relationship. The present is projected backward and forward, thus creating a static, eternal, nonreflective present.

When the more affectionate side of the psychological plane "reappears," the patient often feels that he has "overreacted" or has been "paranoid" and now reinterprets the past and recreates the therapist in a new light. Very frequently, the patient simply does not remember feeling other than he does at present. For example, the patient forgets ever having felt shocked and frightened by the therapist's "gross incompetence" when the therapist forgot the name of the patient's girlfriend. (In Chapter 5, an extended clinical account will be given of massive negation of the history of shared experience that accompanies a patient's psychotic decompensation.)

For the patient relying heavily on splitting, the good (loved) therapist and the bad (feared and hated) therapist are different people. The good therapist can never be disappointing, because as soon as he is disappointing, it is no longer he (the good therapist) with whom the patient is dealing. By definition, it could not have been the loved and loving therapist. Similarly, in a state of mind in which processes of splitting predominate, one's hostile self feels discontinuous from one's loving self, i.e., one does not experience oneself as the same person in different affective states.

The countertransference experience of the therapist when a patient utilizes a splitting defense frequently has a disturbingly discontinuous quality that reflects the patient's emotional discontinuity. When the patient consciously and unconsciously treats the therapist as two or more distinctly different people, a corresponding disruption of the continuity of experience of self is engendered in the therapist. This very frequently results in amnesia on the part of the therapist about events earlier in a given session, or in previous sessions. In a sense the patient "creates" the therapist, not only in phantasy, but also in reality, in that the patient emotionally draws upon the therapist according to the dominant transference configurations.

There is a suggestive parallel between this understanding of splitting in the paranoid-schizoid position and the conclusions that T. G. R. Bower (1971) has drawn from his neonatal observational research:

> According to these studies, it seems that infants less than 16 weeks old live in a world articulated in terms of solids that are stably arranged in space according to their location, with a constancy of existence when they occlude one another. It is, however, a grossly overpopulated world. An object becomes a different object as soon as it moves to a new location. In this world, every object is unique. The infant must cope with a very large number of objects, when only one is really there. (pp. 37–38)

This physical discontinuity of objects when the objects are moved seems to parallel the emotional discontinuity of self and object in different affective "positions" in the paranoid-schizoid state. The infant's world in this phase of development becomes cluttered with emotionally different objects that are, from the point of view of an outside observer, a single object.

Summary

The Kleinian conception of the paranoid-schizoid position is a formulation of the infant's first foothold in the psychological sphere. This position involves a mode of generating and organizing experience in which experience is predominantly of an impersonal, nonreflective nature (i.e., experience of self that has little quality of "I-ness"). Thoughts and feelings are not personal creations; they are events that happen. One does not interpret one's experience; one reacts to it with a high degree of automaticity.

One's symbols do not reflect a layering of personal meanings to be interpreted and understood; one's symbols are what they stand for. This is the realm of things in themselves.

The principal mode of managing danger is splitting, a rearranging of things in themselves in an effort to separate the endangered from the endangering. Projective identification is an elaboration of the process of splitting in which one uses another person to experience at a distance that which one is unwilling or unable to experience oneself.

Splitting allows the infant, child or adult, to love safely and hate safely, by establishing discontinuity between loved and feared aspects of self and object. Without such discontinuity, the infant could not feed safely and would die. Basic to the state of being characterizing the paranoid-schizoid position is the continual rewriting of history in the service of maintaining discontinuities of loving and hating aspects of self and object. It is essential that only one emotional plane exist at a time. Otherwise, object relations become contaminated and, as a result, unbearably complex for the primitive psyche.

4

The Depressive Position and the Birth of the Historical Subject

Klein was able to make it clear . . . how the capacity for concern and to feel guilty is an achievement. . . . This is Klein's most important contribution in my opinion, and I think it ranks with Freud's concept of the Oedipus complex.

—*Donald Winnicott*

The paranoid-schizoid and depressive positions are Klein's conceptualization of psychological organizations that generate distinctive realms of experience or states of being. One does not leave the paranoid-schizoid position behind at the "threshold" of the depressive position; rather, one establishes more or less sucessfully a dialectical relationship between the two, a relationship in which each state creates, preserves, and negates the other, just as the conscious and unconscious mind do in Freud's topographic model.

The understanding of the depressive position that will be presented in this chapter builds upon ideas introduced by Klein, but substantially goes beyond that which is explicit in Klein's writing. Melanie Klein was interested primarily in mental contents and as a result left relatively unexplored the implications of her theory for a psychoanalytic conception of fundamental background states of being.

The Transition into the Depressive Position

As discussed in the previous chapter, the paranoid-schizoid position is a mode of generating experience that is impersonal and automatic. Danger and safety are managed by means of rendering experience discontinuous (by means of splitting) and by ejecting into another person unacceptable or endangered aspects of self (by means of projective identification). The paranoid-schizoid position involves a nonreflective state of being; one's thoughts and feelings are events that merely happen.

The depressive position constitutes an entirely different realm of experience from that which constitutes the paranoid-schizoid position. Entering into the depressive position involves a monumental psychological advance. The concept of a developmental line (A. Freud, 1965) does not adequately capture the nonlinear nature of the shift that occurs, nor is it analogous to the piecing together of a jigsaw puzzle, slowly but surely creating a whole out of the sum of the parts (as in Glover's [1968] conception of the early development of the ego from ego nuclei). A more apt analogy may be drawn from physics: Elements and conditions accumulate, leading to the achievement of a critical mass, at which point a new state, built upon, but qualitatively different from that which preceded it, emerges in a form that could not have been anticipated by looking at the sum of the ingredients (see Spitz's [1959] genetic field theory).

While the transition between these two modes or positions has qualities of a quantum leap, it must also be kept in mind that the paranoid-schizoid and depressive positions are processes and not static entities. It is therefore misleading to talk about the "achievement of the depressive position." It would be more accurate to say that one has begun to function to some extent in the mode of the depressive position, keeping in mind that this mode is undergoing continual development over the course of one's life and that operation in this mode always presupposes simultaneous operation in the mode of the paranoid-schizoid position.

From a Kleinian perspective (as elaborated by Bion [1962a, 1963, 1967]), the psychological-interpersonal process of projective identification is one of the principal vehicles (in association with psycho-physiologic maturation and a predominance of good experience) by which movement is made from the paranoid-schizoid position to the depressive position. The infant's object world in the paranoid-schizoid position consists of part-objects that interact along lines predetermined by the two major instinctual codes. Actual experience, unless modified by the process of projective identification, will simply confirm the infant's polarized preconceptions of absolute danger and serene safety.

Projective identification allows for an exit from the initially closed system of the infant's psychic reality. The interaction with the mother that constitutes projective

identification makes it possible for the infant to modify his
instinctual preconceptions, i.e., to learn from experience.
An infant's nonreflective anticipation of sadistic rejection
by the mother may be tempered through the maternal
"containment process" (Bion, 1962a, 1962b). The idealized object undergoes modification in a similar way. Good
experience and maturation do not fully account for the
transformation of part-objects; it is the modification of the
quality of the infant's receptivity and meaning-generating
system which occurs in the interaction that constitutes
projective identification,[1] that makes it possible for the
infant to discriminate new experience from that which had
been anticipated.

The Kleinians (Klein, 1935, 1958; Segal, 1957, 1964)
invoke a combination of maturational factors and actual
experience to account for the integration of good and bad
part-objects. The maturational factors include a diminu-
tion of instinctual drive intensity and an unfolding of
cognitive capacities, including the stabilization of the capacity for reality testing and memory. With these maturational changes as a foundation, the integration of part-
objects and parts of self becomes possible when good
experience predominates. Satisfactory experience with objects enhances the infant's feeling of attachment to and
love from internal good objects and diminishes the infant's fear of bad objects. As this occurs, bad objects need
not be as forcefully extruded by means of projection and
projective identification. The result is a decrease in persecutory anxiety. The good object need not be kept quite
so emotionally separate from the bad object and gradually,

[1]As discussed in Chapter 2, Klein was only minimally aware of these
interpersonal implications of the concept of projective identification.

as this process proceeds, good and bad aspects of self and good and bad part-objects can be experienced as different qualities of a single whole object and a single whole self.[2]

The Development of Subjectivity

In the process of moving from part-object relatedness into whole-object relatedness and from split-self experience to a continuity of experience of self, the infant becomes human and potentially humane. In attempting to understand the transformation in the quality of experience that becomes possible in the depressive position, one is struck by the wide array of developmental advances that underlie this metamorphosis, e.g., an enhanced capacity for self-object differentiation, the development of the capacity for symbol formation, increased capacities for affective modu-

---

[2]Klein's explanation of the achievement of whole object relations is a mechanical one and does not address the question of what has changed to allow the radical transformation of the quality of experience achieved in the whole object relatedness of the depressive position. Klein's (1935, 1940) thinking is hampered by the fact that she is dealing entirely in the conceptual vocabulary of mental contents. Her explanation is a quantitative one in which successive deletions of affective and ideational extremes allow a "coming together" of good and bad internal parts to form an internally cohesive whole object and whole ego. I believe that Klein's failure to adequately develop a conceptualization of the intrapersonal and interpersonal matrix within which mental contents exist left her with insufficient terms to account for the transformation that she is addressing. A fuller understanding of the nature of the radical developmental transformation in question depends upon an understanding of Winnicott's conception of potential space. The discussion of this contribution to the psychoanalytic dialogue will be deferred until Chapters 7, 8, and 9.

lation, reality testing, and memory. No single developmental advance accounts for the shift in the infant's state of being that will be described. Unfortunately, one cannot address the developmental whole without considering the parts separately, thereby giving the illusion of one part leading to another sequentially. In actuality, each aspect of development creates the conditions necessary for the emergence of the others.

I will begin with a discussion of the development of subjectivity, the experience of "I-ness," which is a concomitant of the differentiation of symbol and symbolized. In the paranoid-schizoid position, the symbol and the symbolized were emotionally interchangeable, leading to an immediacy of experience manifested in extreme concreteness of thought, entrapment in the manifest, and delusional quality of experience (including transference experience). The symbol is what it represents. At the threshold of the depressive position, the maturity of the infant's psychological organization has reached the point where a structural shift becomes possible. When symbol and symbolized become distinguishable, a sense of "I-ness" fills the space between symbol and symbolized. This "I" is the interpreter of one's symbols, the mediator between one's thoughts and that which one is thinking about, the intermediary between the self and one's lived sensory experience. One might well ask whether the sense of "I-ness" makes it possible to differentiate between symbol and symbolized or whether the differentiation of symbol and symbolized allows for the emergence of a sense of "I-ness." I would view both as true: each makes the other possible, but neither is the cause of the other in a linear sense.

At the moment that the infant becomes capable of experiencing himself as the interpreter of his perceptions, the infant as subject is born. All experience from that point on is a personal creation (unless there is subsequent regression). In the paranoid-schizoid position, everything is what it is (i.e., events speak for themselves), whereas in the depressive position, nothing is simply what it appears to be (events do not have intrinsic meaning). In the depressive position an event is what one makes of it; its significance lies in the interpretation one gives it.[3] (It must be kept in mind that the psychological state of being just described always coexists with the paranoid-schizoid position wherein perceptions are experienced as things in themselves.)

When the infant becomes an interpreting subject, he can for the first time project that state of mind into his sense of the other and consider the possibility that other people experience feelings and thoughts in much the same way. Awareness of the possibility that another person is a subject as well as an object creates the conditions wherein the infant can feel concern for another person.[4]

When the infant becomes capable of feeling concern for another as a whole and separate person, i.e., a living human being, he then becomes capable of guilt and the

---

[3]Even though one interprets one's experience in the depressive position, each individual as an isolate cannot create meaning. Meanings are created intersubjectively in the context of one's family and culture, with language utilized as the vehicle for a shared system of symbols and understandings (see Habermas, 1968).

[4]Winnicott (1954–1955) refers to this developmental advance as the infant's development of the capacity for "ruth" (p. 265), which contrasts with the state of "ruthlessness" that exists prior to the development of the recognition of the other as a living person. Ruthlessness for Winnicott is not hostile in intent; rather, it simply reflects the infant's inability to have empathy for the mother with regard to the impact of his intense neediness and dependence on her.

wish to make reparations. It is possible for him to feel bad about the way in which he has hurt another person (in reality or in phantasy) and to a large degree to be able to distinguish between real and imagined harm.

There are major differences between the experience of destructiveness and restitution in the paranoid-schizoid and that in the depressive position. In the former the object of one's aggression is an impersonal object that is not felt to have feelings or subjectivity, because the infant himself is devoid of subjectivity. The paranoid-schizoid position is a magical state in which one need not be concerned about destroying one's enemy because one is able omnipotently to re-create what one has destroyed if one wishes to restore it.[5]

From the vantage point of this understanding of the experiential state characterizing the paranoid-schizoid position, it is possible to understand why the principal anxiety of the paranoid-schizoid position is not the fear of

[5]The distinction here between the subjectivity and objectivity of the other is to some extent captured in the following political allegory. It has been suggested that "the button" for launching missiles carrying nuclear warheads be surgically implanted under the skin of a Secret Service agent who would accompany the President at all times. If the President decides to enter the country into a nuclear war, he would have to cut open the skin of the Secret Service man in order to "press the button." It is with considerable shame that we admit to ourselves that in some sense we recoil more from the idea of cutting open the Secret Service man than we do at the prospect of the destruction of (unmentioned) millions of people. In our identification with the President in this phantasied scene, the Secret Service agent is experienced as a man who has to be looked at, talked to, and touched, and therefore is alive as a human being; the millions whom we do not visualize in this phantasy are not alive for us as human beings and therefore cannot suffer pain and cannot die.

death but the fear of "nihilation."[6] One cannot die if one is not alive. Chairs do not die nor are they hurt; they are damaged or destroyed. In the paranoid-schizoid position, there is no immutable history created intersubjectively and preserved in subjective memory. Instead of dying, one disappears without a trace. In contrast, a death at the end of a life is both more and less absolute. It is less absolute because a person may anticipate that he will continue to exist in the people who have been influenced by shared experience or by the symbols that he has created (and which have been interpreted by others) to reflect his individuality. Paradoxically, the idea of death from the point of view of the paranoid-schizoid position is less absolute than it is in the context of the depressive position. In the paranoid-schizoid position absence is never permanent; there is always the possibility of omnipotent re-creation of the absent object.

While the principal anxiety of the paranoid-schizoid position is the fear of nihilation, the principal anxiety of the depressive position is the fear of the loss of the object. The lost object is experienced as a whole and separate human being whom one fears one has driven away, harmed, or killed. Mourning is the working through of depressive anxiety; depression and manic-depressive illness are pathological formations generated in response to

[6]Kojève's (1934–1935) neologism *néantir* translated by Nichols (1960) as "nihilate" seems to me to capture the idea of the negation of one's existence. The term *annihilate* heavily connotes violent and destructive negation of one's existence or the existence of the other. In this book, I will use either *nihilate* or *annihilate*, depending upon whether the act of destruction is central to the activity described.

depressive anxiety. (The manic defense against depressive anxiety will be discussed later in this chapter.)

The Management of Danger in the Depressive Position

The objectivity (nonreflectiveness) of the self in the paranoid-schizoid position accounts for the mode of managing danger that is utilized in that state of being. In a world of things in themselves (including the self as object), it is not possible to secure safety through an understanding or compromise in which each of two or more parties (subjects) are changed (intersubjectively) in order to make their peace. In a realm of objects (as opposed to subjects) safety is attained through quantitative shifts and magical all-or-nothing transformations. One achieves safety in relation to internal danger by magically placing the danger outside of oneself; one protects oneself against persecutory objects by acquiring a greater army of good objects; one protects an endangered aspect of self by magically transforming another person into a repository for that aspect of self, thus preserving oneself in the form of another with whom one maintains a connection of identity (projective identification).

The renunciation of omnipotence in the depressive position is integrally connected with the establishment of the separateness of the object from oneself. It is only when one cannot create or magically transform the object that something or someone exists that is not oneself. If there is someone who is not me, whom I cannot create, control, and transform, then I also emerge as a separate person. In the renunciation of omnipotence, the real is created as an entity separate from one's thoughts. In terms of symbol formation, the symbolized (the referent of my thoughts in the real) is for the first time freed from the symbol that I create (my thoughts and feelings about that which I am perceiving). One is freed from the realm of the thing in itself.[7]

Envy and Jealousy

The distinction between envy and jealousy provides specific experiential referents for the preceding discussion of the relationship of the paranoid-schizoid to the depressive position. For Klein (1952c, 1957, 1961), envy is one of the most important manifestations of the death instinct. As a phenomenon of the paranoid-schizoid position; envy is a part-object relationship in which one hates the object for having what one feels one does not have and what one desperately needs. One wishes to steal the envied possession from the object and spoil whatever one cannot steal.

> During the psychotherapy of a severely disturbed patient, the therapist became pregnant. The patient, Ms. W., blandly denied having any feelings about this, but developed a terrifying feeling that she would discover an aborted fetus in each toilet she was about to use. During the same period, Ms. W. found it unbearably painful to shop in stores because she could buy only a few items, leaving so much in the store that the few items she was able to purchase felt

[7]This space between one's omnipotence and that which lies outside of one's omnipotence is Winnicott's (1971e) "potential space" and was largely unrecognized and unexplored by Klein. This aspect of early development will be examined in detail in the discussion of Winnicott's work on potential space (see especially Chapter 8).

like a mockery of her. It was with great effort that she refrained from stealing.

The patient's unconscious wish to have all of the therapist completely to herself led to intense, unconscious envy of the therapist's baby (and, secondarily, of the therapist for having the baby). The patient unconsciously wished to kill the baby because the baby possessed what the patient wanted. In addition, Ms. W. wished to spoil the envied possession of the baby and of the therapist.

Envy involves a two-person, part-object relationship, whereas jealousy is understood as a three-person, whole-object-related phenomenon of the depressive position. Jealousy is a manifestation of the individual's wish to be loved in the way he feels that another person (the object of jealousy) is loved by a third person. It involves a degree of empathy with the other person (putting oneself into the place of the object of jealousy without losing oneself in the other) and a sense of the third person as a whole and separate other whom one can imagine being loved by and loving.

Envy involves not only hatred of the object for possessing the good, but also hatred of the good itself, because the owner and the owned are emotionally equivalent. Jealousy is a far more complex feeling state (at core an ambivalently loving set of feelings) that involves anger at being excluded from a love relationship. One wishes to love and be loved, but feels shut out of that experience by another person, who is felt to be enjoying that love relationship in one's stead. Jealousy is built upon a series of wish–fear compromises designed in large part to deal with problems of ambivalence: One dares not engage in a love relationship, and yet one does so vicariously through an identification with the object of jealousy; one dares not directly hate the love object, instead hating a displacement object (the object of jealousy); one fears the fantasied destructiveness of sexual excitement and modulates it through the use of an intermediary; one disguises violently intrusive voyeuristic wishes in the feeling that one has been forced into the position of the intensely interested observer. In jealousy, these wishes and fears are feelings generated by a subject. One's feelings are *potentially* experienceable as one's own, even though one may vigorously attempt to disown these feelings by means of repression, projection, denial, displacement, or projective identification.

Having schematically described envy and jealousy as if they were separable feeling states, it is important to emphasize that these emotions represent coexisting ends of a single gradient, always standing in a hierarchial relationship to each other. Neither envy nor jealousy is encountered in pure form. Each psychological state in which these feelings play a role must be understood in terms of an interplay of these two forms of relatedness.

The Creation of History

In the depressive position, the infant increasingly renounces the power to magically re-create that which he has damaged or destroyed. In this new emotional context, the infant develops a new quality of object relatedness that involves the wish to make up for what he has done. He cannot nihilate the past and start again. The historical self exists for the first time.

The experience of history is a distinctly human phenomenon (Kojève, 1934–1935). Animals undergo evolutionary progression in which biologically determined response patterns are played out. History requires the capacity for self-reflection. In the absence of this capacity, animals live only in the present. Only man self-reflectively can remember who he was after he is changed by his experience in the world. The infant in the depressive position begins to experience both himself and the other person as largely the same people they were before the infant, for example, hurt the mother (in phantasy or in reality). They do not become different people, but an additional event has been added to their common experience.

In contrast, in the paranoid-schizoid position, the past is constantly changing: each new event radically changes all previous ones. The present is immediately projected onto all previous experience thus nihilating the past. The past becomes merely a fluid extension of the present. When the borderline patient becomes angry at the therapist, all previous experience is viewed as a deception on the part of the therapist. (See Chapter 5 for clinical examples of such rewriting of history.)

In the depressive position, the infant no longer has access to the kind of Orwellian rewriting of history that is possible in the paranoid-schizoid position. In the depressive state of being, when one feels that one has hurt another person, one is stuck with that fact. One cannot negate or rewrite history, one cannot obliterate the fact that an event of a given nature has occurred. One can try to make it up to the other person, knowing full well that this one does not change the past. The development of the capacity to make reparations of a nonmagical type is one of the hallmarks of the depressive position.

Only when another person can no longer be magically re-created (e. g., by wholesale substitution of a new mothering figure for an absent one), does it become possible to miss someone who is away or to mourn someone who has died or who has left permanently. When the other can be experienced as having an existence separate from one's own, it becomes possible to be with that person and be away from that person in an entirely different way from that which had been possible previously. One cannot leave or be left by another person if one has not allowed the other person to be present and alive as a human being. By analogy, one cannot leave a place one has never been to (see Searles, 1982). The danger to which one exposes oneself in entering the world of human beings (i.e., in achieving the whole-object relatedness of the depressive position) is that of feeling concern for people whom one does not control. Therefore, one opens oneself to the possibility of being left (physically and emotionally) by another person. The feeling of loneliness is generated and maintained for the first time in the depressive position. The experiencing of loneliness over time requires that the individual tolerate the presence of an absence without filling the void with projections of the self, through hallucinatory wish fulfillment or the construction of a paranoid world in which persecutory objects provide constant company.

The principal anxiety of the depressive position, the anxiety that one will harm or drive away the person whom one loves, could not possibly have arisen in the paranoid-schizoid position even though there were phantasies of annihilating the object in that state. In the paranoid-schizoid position, the people who are loved and the people who are hated are different people. This is a restatement from a different vantage point of the idea that the process of splitting in the paranoid-schizoid position allows the infant to avoid the dilemma of hating the loved person and loving the hated person.

From the perspective developed thus far, it can be seen that the term *depressive position* is a misleading one. The term *historical position* better represents what is normative in the achievement of this psychological organization. Mourning rather than depression is the psychological process by which previous object ties are relinquished. Historical memory is itself a form of mourning in that it acknowledges the fact that the past (and the object ties that constitute one's past) no longer exist in their earlier form. As Freud (1911-1915) pointed out in his technical papers, transference is an act of repeating instead of remembering and is therefore always a resistance to relinquishing the object ties constituting the transference. Analysis of the transference is in part a process of transforming a repetition into a memory and in this sense is aimed at expanding the historicity of the depressive position. The process of transforming enactment into remembering (the elaboration of feelings in a symbolic realm with a historical dimension) and the sustaining of those feelings over time is at the heart of what Freud (1932) meant by: *"Wo Es war, soll Ich werden"* ("Where it was, there I shall be").

Responsibility for Action in the Depressive Position

The act of avowing one's role as the interpreter of experience is an important form of taking responsibility for one's actions. The counterpart of this experience of being responsible for one's actions (including mental activity) is the experience of freedom. It is only when one has empowered oneself with the responsibility for one's actions that one can make choices in which one feels varying degrees of freedom, depending upon the perceived importance of limiting internal and external factors.

Schafer's (1976) action language is the fully articulated language of the depressive position. It is a way of speaking in which the subject's responsibility for his thoughts, feelings, and behavior is fully acknowledged. For example, Schafer believes that reification of affect and motivation serves to disavow the subject's position as active agent in relation to his psychological activity and behavior. In an unconscious effort to disavow his responsibility for what he has angrily done, a patient might say, "The anger was building up in me to the point that I exploded" or "I don't know what made me do that." In an action-disclaiming stance, patients unconsciously protest, "'Allow us our illusions of ignorance, passivity and helplessness. We dare not acknowledge that we are masters in our own house.'" (p. 154).

In the fully developed depressive position (a never-achieved ideal state), we are subjects aware of our responsibility for our thoughts, feelings, and behavior. However, from the perspective developed in this chapter, the depressive position coexists dialectically with the paranoid-schizoid position. When the individual is functioning predominantly in a paranoid-schizoid mode, he is to a considerable degree lived by experience. It is therefore inaccurate to use language that implies otherwise. Action language fails to reflect the nature of the structure of the paranoid-schizoid component of all psychological states, a component that is predominant in primitive mental states. The individual's inability to fully experience himself as "the master of his own house," is not simply a reflection of a "frightened, resistant, action-disclaiming stance" (p. 154).

To the extent that there is not yet a subject in the paranoid-schizoid position, one cannot possibly take responsibility for emotions that present themselves to a nonsubjective self as forces and objects impinging upon or emanating from a self as object. This experience of self as object is not simply a defense; it is an inevitable component of psychological development and an ongoing facet of psychological organization. One does not leave behind this mode of organizing experience; one incorporates it into the mature dialectical relationship of the paranoid-schizoid and depressive states of being. From this perspective, Schafer's action language overstates the degree to which we are subjects and underestimates the degree to which the self forever remains an object. The it (id) never fully becomes I (ego), nor would we want it to. We need language other than action language to talk with and about that aspect of being.

The Manic Defense

Patients who have unstably achieved the depressive position often rely on a specific form of defense that Klein (1935, 1952c) terms the *manic process* or *defense*. This defense (more accurately thought of as a group of defenses) is an in-between phenomenon, incorporating elements of the psychic organization of both the paranoid-schizoid and the depressive positions. It is a defense against depressive anxiety (the fear of the loss of an object that is experienced as whole and separate), but employs modes of defense that are characteristic of the paranoid-schizoid position (e.g., splitting, denial, projection, introjection, idealization, projective identification, and omnipotent thinking). The manic process involves a regression to a state of being in which subjectivity, historicity, the experience of psychic reality, and the capacity for mature symbol formation are all greatly compromised. The patient who utilizes manic defenses does not live in a world of layered symbolic meanings where feelings, thoughts, and events can be understood. The hypomanic or manic patient lives in a world of action where events speak for themselves and are dealt with reactively. The manic defense is by no means used only by manic-depressive patients any more than projection is a defense utilized exclusively by paranoid patients. However, the manic defense is seen in its most extreme form in manic and hypomanic states. Once one has begun to consolidate the psychic organization of the depressive position, the manic defense becomes a part of the normative defensive repertoire.

The manic defense involves the denial of one's dependence on other people (Klein, 1935, 1963b). This denial is reinforced by the unconscious phantasy of omnipotent control over the object, which phantasy protects the individual against the anxiety of being abandoned by the object: One need not fear the loss of an object over which one feels one has absolute control. Moreover, contempt for the object serves to insulate the individual from loss, since one need not be concerned by the loss of the despised, worthless object (see Segal, 1964).

> I was asked to consult on a hospitalized man in his early forties who had been involuntarily committed to the hospital two days earlier. The patient, Mr. L., walked haughtily into the interview room and immediately began to complain about the "smallness of mind" of the ward nursing staff. He felt that the opportunity to speak with a physician might be more interesting for him. He spoke in a loud, vaguely

threatening voice that clearly conveyed how explo-
sively angry he could get if he were made to feel that
he was not totally in control of the situation. He used
French and German idioms to express the precise
meanings he was looking for. Mr. L. told me that he
had been a graduate student in comparative literature
at a prestigious university, but for financial reasons
had been unable to complete his studies. He was
avoiding talking about anything that might lead me to
ask him why he was in the hospital. That subject
would have shattered the illusion that the two of us
were simply "educated men" striking up a conversation. Despite his bluster, there was something quite
poignant about this man's fragility; he seemed to be
silently pleading with me throughout the interview
not to rob him of his illusions.

   The mood of the hour shifted when he asked me
how many foreign languages I spoke. I hesitated and
said that I hoped he would allow me not to take his
question literally since . . . He interrupted me before
I could finish the thought by saying that I was ob-
viously attempting to conceal the true depths of my
ignorance and that he had no more interest in talking
with me. It seemed to me that Mr. L. felt that my
reluctance to answer his question and the likelihood
that I was about to offer an interpretation represented an effort to flaunt my power, to diminish
him, and to take control of the interview. At that
point, he picked up a magazine from the table between us and began thumbing through it with a
feigned air of relaxation. For the next fifteen minutes
he acted as if he were alone in the room, especially
when I attempted to talk to him. When I finally told
him that our time was up he gave no response at all

and we sat there in silence for several minutes. At that point he tossed his magazine onto the table, saying, "It's too hot in this room; I'm getting out of here." He left the room, but I sensed that he had not gone far. When I opened the door to the hallway, he was standing very close to the door. I said that I, too, felt that there was more to say to each other and that we could talk together the following day if he liked. With his head down, he slowly walked away.

In this interview, Mr. L. relied heavily on a set of manic defenses that included denial (of my ending of the meeting and of the nature of our relationship), a grandiose twinship phantasy (the two of us as superior men), contempt, and phantasied omnipotent control (reflected in his domination of the flow and direction of the interview). The patient also relied on projective identification; through this process it was I who carried the patient's disowned feelings of trepidation and of sadness (until the interview was over). Despite the primitive nature of the defenses being utilized, it was clear that Mr. L. was attempting to protect himself against painful loss of self-esteem and loss of connectedness with another person. This patient would not allow the disaster of a severed attachment to happen to him, and yet he could not entirely keep himself from yearning for the company of another person on whom he unconsciously hoped he could depend.

The use of manic defenses is rarely as dramatic as in the case just described. It must be reiterated that manic defenses constitute a component of the defensive repertoire of all individuals. For example, a neurotic patient who was experiencing fear of abandonment in the context of a maternal transference would retreat from his customary (relatively mature) mode of object relatedness and would begin treating the therapist in a condescending fashion, e.g., by becoming grandiose (in a disguised way) about his own accomplishments in comparison with those of the therapist. At times, this patient's manifestations of the manic defense were extremely subtle, initially observable only in the hint of contempt in his tone of voice or an air of nonchalance about a delay in paying his bill.

The Achievement of Ambivalence

I would like at this point to focus the discussion on the psychological-interpersonal processess involved in the developmental movement toward the capacity for ambivalence. The idea of the integration of good and bad part-objects, although heuristically appealing, does not fully describe what is involved in this developmental advance. Ambivalence is not simply a matter of consciously and unconsciously loving and hating the same object at a given moment, for this might well describe a very primitive undifferentiated state of affairs often seen in schizophrenic patients. Under such circumstances, the schizophrenic patient is unable to determine whether his feelings are of a loving or hating nature since these emotions are "all mixed-up together." There is a physical correlate that regularly accompanies this failure to differentiate feelings: the patient is unable to distinguish between different physical/emotional sensations, e.g., between hunger and sexual excitement or between nausea and anger.

Likewise, it is not sufficient to say that in ambivalence one hates consciously and loves unconsciously or vice versa, because this does not address the relationship of that which is hated to that which is loved. The critical achievement in the attainment of ambivalence is the fact that the person one hates is the *same person* whom one has loved and unconsciously still loves and hopes to openly love again. There is no rewriting of history; there is no feeling that one has uncovered the truth of which one was previously only dimly aware. When one hates, the love that one had felt is still real and is present in the history that one shares with the person hated. Therefore, the feeling of sadness is integral to ambivalence because nothing can be taken back. In the paranoid-schizoid position sadness is simply not part of one's emotional vacabulary. How could it be? Everything is taken back when a new emotional state is entered. The feelings of sadness involved in mourning, guilt, and the renunciation of omnipotence are among the "prices" one pays for becoming human in the way that one does in the depressive position. The "depression" of the depressive position is more accurately thought of as a feeling of sadness involved in the acknowledgment that history cannot be rewritten. One is vulnerable to loss of loved objects whom one cannot omnipotently control and whom one cannot re-create or restore. There is sadness in the knowledge that one can attempt to make up for the harm one has done, but one cannot change the fact that it has been done. Further, the sadness of the depressive position is connected with the acceptance of the fact that one's most passionate longings deriving from one's early object relations were not fully realized and will not be fulfilled in the way that one had wished. As will be discussed later, central among these "renunciations" (perhaps better described as regretful resignations) are one's oedipal longings.

The phenomenon of mature transference (as opposed to delusional or psychotic transference described by Searles,

1963 and Little, 1958) makes the sadness of the depressive position bearable. For just as one cannot take back the past, the past can never be taken away. The form of transference possible in the depressive position allows one to perpetuate, to have again, important parts of what one has experienced with people whom one has lost through absence, death, emotional unavailability, or psychological change. This transference experience (both within and outside of the therapeutic setting) makes tolerable the pain of loss. One does not magically replace earlier objects; one experiences with the new person feelings like those one felt with the previous person. In this way one does not have to give up entirely past experience with significant objects. One may have to give up people whom one has lost, but one does not have to give up entirely one's experience with those people. One knows that the person in the present (the transference object, who is also experienced as a real person in his own right) and the original object are different. But this knowledge is tolerable because the new experience (unconsciously) feels connected with the earlier one, and in this way earlier experience is preserved.

A very important distinction can be made at this point: *Transference in the depressive position is an attempted preservation of a feeling state from a past relationship; transference in the paranoid-schizoid position is an attempted preservation of the lost object itself.* In psychotic or delusional transferences, the patient experiences the present object and the original object as identical, despite "inconsequential" dissimilarities of sex, age, race, and so on. In the paranoid-schizoid position history is constantly being rewritten and this rewriting can easily include matters of age, sex, or race.

We can now see from a new vantage point that the capacity for the type of transference achieved in the depressive position provides the potential for making tolerable the idea of one's own death. Just as one comes to feel that one's experience with lost objects is never entirely lost, it is also possible to come to feel that others' experience with oneself and the symbols one has created may not be entirely lost after one's death.

The Depressive Position and the Oedipus Complex

Psychological conflict generated in the depressive position is of a distinctly different type than that seen in the paranoid-schizoid position. The father whom one wishes dead is the same person whom one loves and would not want to lose. In the depressive position, phantasies of omnipotently annihilating one's rival no longer provide a satisfactory solution to a problem in a human relationship. In normal development, a new form of defense is generated in this setting. The new defense preserves the continuity of the history of the object relationship even as it wards off awareness of an aspect of the relationship. The new defense, repression, is based on an unconscious belief that "what I don't know won't hurt me, and forgetting won't hurt [or change the identity of] the forgotten." One's relationship with one's father, including one's murderous anger toward him when he is felt to be acting selfishly, unfairly, and tyrannically, is preserved unconsciously. In the act of repression one changes what one knows (more accurately, what one avows knowing), not who one is or who the other person is. History is not rewritten in repression as it is in splitting; rather, history (which is a combination of memory and phantasy) is "buried" and thereby preserved.

It is often incorrectly thought that the oedipal phase of development follows the depressive position. Such a conception mixes qualitatively different developmental constructs. The achievement of the depressive position is the entry into the world of whole object relations, i.e., the world of subjective human beings each possessing an immutable past and a relatively fixed history. These persons can be cared about and mourned for; one can feel guilt and remorse toward them. The relationship of the depressive position to the oedipal situation is the relationship between container and content, each shaping and influencing the other.

As discussed in Chapter 2, the Oedipus complex for Freud is not simply one of many psychological contents; it is a phylogenetically determined nucleus for the creation and organization of sexual and aggressive meanings. For this reason the Oedipus complex is treated by Freud as a cornerstone of psychoanalysis, a fundamental theory of symbolic meanings, a developmental theory, a theory of pathogenesis, and a theory of therapy. In this chapter, I will make a few introductory comments toward a discussion of this important topic.

Klein (1945, 1952c, 1955) viewed the Oedipus complex as a phenomenon of the depressive position. Klein's developmental timetable is based on a synchronic as well as a diachronic view of development. Stages of development follow one another sequentially and, at the same time, all psychosexual stages coexist from the beginning. For example, in speaking of the early development of the girl, Klein (1932a) writes:

Since the oral frustration she has suffered from her mother has stimulated all her other erotogenic zones as well and has aroused her genital tendencies and desires in regard to her father's penis, the latter becomes the object of her oral, urethral, anal and genital impulses, *all at the same time* [italics added]. (p. 272)

At another point, Klein (1932a) elaborates:

. . . In my opinion, the early equation of the penis with the breast is ushered in by the frustration she [the girl] has suffered from the breast in early childhood, and at once exerts a powerful influence on her and greatly affects the whole trend of her development. I also believe that the equation of penis and breast, accompanied as it is by a "displacement from above downward," activates the oral, receptive qualities of the female genital at an early age and prepares for the vagina to receive the penis. It thus clears the way for the little girl's Oedipus tendencies—though these, it is true, do not unfold their full power until much later—and lays the foundation of her sexual development. (p. 271, fn.)

Bibring (1947) has described Klein's thinking as a development theory in which "spreading" (p. 73) occurs between levels of libidinal development, prior to a time at which one ordinarily conceives of the "later" development phases (e.g., urethral, anal, and genital) as having been reached. Development is understood by Klein not only as a process of sequential unfolding but also as a process of "precipitation" (Bibring 1947, p. 83), i.e., the early calling into play of aspects of all levels of libidinal development. The unconscious, according to Klein, is not limited to a linear, sequential mode of maturation or development. (See also Boyer, 1967, for a lucid description of the synchronic aspect of Kleinian developmental theory.)

Oedipal experience originating in the fourth to sixth months of life is organized by the child as a mixture of oral, urethral, anal, and genital phantasies (Klein, 1928, 1932b, 1952c). These include, for example, conceptions of parental intercourse as involving the mother's eating up the father with her mouth/vagina; phantasies of fecal babies inside the mother; phantasies of the child enviously penetrating the mother and destroying the father/penis/ rival-sibling-babies inside the mother. (For a detailed account of the nature of these phantasies, see Klein, 1932b.) As I have discussed in Chapter 2, the content of these phantasies (that arise prior to experience-derived knowledge of sexual anatomy and sexual intercourse) is understood by Klein (1932b, 1952c) to be part of one's phylogenetic inheritance. The intense debate over this aspect of the Kleinian developmental timetable and the debate about the nature of the contents of the child's sexual and oedipal phantasies (see Bibring, 1947; Glover, 1945; Waelder, 1937; Zetzel, 1956), has, I believe, prevented a full discussion and exploration of the implications of Klein's more basic proposal that the Oedipus complex arises in and is resolved within the context of a depressive organization. In what follows I will discuss my own understanding of the implications of the "depressive" (i.e., historical) context for the oedipal drama. The ideas I will present were not explored by Klein.

The critical emotional capacities involved in the resolution of the oedipal situation are the capacity for subjectivity, historicity, object love, ambivalence, mourning, guilt, and reparation. In the positive oedipal situation for the boy, the child's love for his mother has thrust him into a conflict of subjective desire. He has fallen in love with his mother and unconsciously wishes for genital as well as pregenital sexual relations with her; at the same time he unconsciously feels that the fulfillment of these wishes involves the breaking of sacred laws (Eliade, 1963; Loewald, 1979). Culturally, these sacred laws (which are communicated unconsciously by the parents) involve the prohibition of incest and of parricide.

In terms of the child's individually generated system of meanings, the idea of sexual intercourse with one's mother involves a regression to an undifferentiated state and therefore a nihilation of oneself and one's mother as separate individuals. In addition to this nihilation of self and other, there is also a wish on the part of the boy to kill his father, mother, and siblings, insofar as they are experienced as getting in the way of the fulfillment of his desires.

Such conflict of desire is not possible in a predominantly paranoid-schizoid state, since there is not yet a subject responsible for his thoughts, feelings, and behavior. When one's thoughts and feelings are experienced as events or forces that simply happen, one cannot be conflicted. One can fear, bemoan, or yearn for specific internal and external events (e.g., a primitive tribesman might beseech the gods for rain or fear the effects of his "evil eye" on his child), but these are not internal conflicts of subjective desire.

The impact of the Oedipus complex on the formation of psychological structure is determined by the child's method of attempting to resolve this conflict of subjective desire. If splitting and reenactment are used as methods of defense against oedipal anxiety, limited psychological change occurs. The child endlessly keeps multiple poles of his conflicted wishes alive simultaneously (e.g., the boy's wish to be his mother's husband and sexual partner and his wish to be her child), and establishes a series of relationships with part-objects embodying each of the aspects of his unrenounced wishes. (See the case of Ms. H. described in Chapter 3 for an example of splitting used to manage oedipal desires.)

When one is able to maintain the whole-object relatedness, subjectivity, and historicity of the depressive position in the face of oedipal conflict, one's unwillingness to violate sacred prohibitions in the acts of incest and parricide outweighs one's desire for the enactment of one's oedipal wishes. The context of this renunciation of oedipal strivings is both intrapsychic and interpersonal. The parents must both accept the child's wishes and protectively prohibit them. The child's unconscious sexual desires must be recognized by the parents in order for the child to experience oedipal love as an important reflection of individuality, separateness, and consolidation of gender identity. The child's parricidal wishes must also be recognized and accepted by the parents, because these, too, are wishes that help establish the foundation for the child's efforts to transcend psychologically his or her identity as a child and eventually become an adult and parent. "In our role as children of our parents, by genuine emancipation [in the process of mastering the Oedipus complex], we do kill something vital in them [our parents]—not all in one blow and not in all respects, but contributing to their dying. As parents of our children we undergo the same fate, unless we diminish them [by not allowing them to grow up]" (Loewald, 1979, p. 395).

But, of course, there is far more to the parental response to the child's Oedipus complex than the recognition (and the particular type of acceptance described by Loewald) of the child's desires. The parents must at the same time assist the child in his efforts at preserving his own and his parents' individual existences, which are threatened by incestuous and parricidal wishes. In order to understand the nature of the role of the parents in this situation, one must differentiate between prohibition and threat. A threat attempts to induce compliance through the induction in the other of a fear of punishment or retaliation. Prohibition need not include threat; a danger sign on an electrical fuse box need not be experienced as threatening. Under proper circumstances, the parents' oedipal prohibitions are offered and recognized as predominantly protective, caretaking injunctions that provide safety in the face of potential object-related dangers. Because the talion principle constitutes an important aspect of paranoid-schizoid morality, the parental prohibitions are universally distorted by the child and experienced in part as threats (of castration and infanticide) that retaliate for the child's sexual and aggressive wishes. To the extent that parental prohibitions are experienced as threats, the child internalizes a primitively punitive superego. Polarization of the punishing and the punished, the endangering and the endangered is a form of splitting that does not involve mourning and does not lead to successful resolution of the Oedipus complex.

On the other hand, when parental prohibitions are unconsciously experienced as caretaking injunctions (albeit to a large extent unwelcome ones), identification with one's prohibiting parents facilitates both the mourning of the lost object relationship (e.g., the girl's romantic, erotic

relationship with her father) and the establishment of
internal safety vis-à-vis one's sexual and aggressive desires. The renunciation of the girl's sexual and romantic
love for her father (or the boy's love of his mother) is not
crisp and absolute (for that would reflect denial) and is
perhaps better described as regretful resignation. The pain
of this mourning is to some extent mitigated by the independence that the child achieves in the process. Oedipal
love, like all acts of falling in love, has an addictive, driven
quality. There is considerable relief for the latency-aged
child in his or her release from the internal pressure of
being in love with a forbidden object. A degree of freedom
from this intense and conflicted set of object relations
allows the child the opportunity to begin to develop a life
separate from his or her parents.

The identification with the prohibiting parents that
underlies the establishment of the superego is motivated
largely by a wish to make reparations to one's parents,
whom one loves and toward whom one feels guilt for one's
murderous and incestuous wishes. In becoming like one's
parents by internalizing their unconscious prohibitions of
one's sexual and aggressive strivings, one attempts to
make up for the fantasied incest and parricide. Paradoxically, through the same identificatory act, one moves
toward completing the process of becoming independent
by providing one's own internal environment of safety.

Summary

The question of what lies "beyond the depressive
position," from the perspective developed in this chapter,
is a question based on a misconception. The "depression"
of the depressive position is not something that is over-

come or worked through in order to get to another phase of development. Feelings of loss, guilt, sadness, remorse, compassion, empathy, and loneliness are burdens that are unavoidable if one is to become a historical human being in the depressive position. What one gains is subjective humanness and the potential to be free to make choices. This is not a dilemma that one resolves: one is stuck with it, with all of its advantages and disadvantages, unless one regressively flees from it into the refuge and imprisonment of the paranoid-schizoid position or through the use of manic defenses.

---5---

Between the
Paranoid-Schizoid and
the Depressive Position

I thought that Argos and I participated in different universes; I thought that our perceptions were the same, but that he combined them in another way and made other objects of them; I thought that perhaps there were no objects for him, only a vertiginous and continuous play of extremely brief impressions. I thought of a world without memory, without time; I considered the possibility of a language without nouns, a language of impersonal verbs or indeclinable epithets.

—*Jorge Luis Borges, "The Immortal"*

In this chapter I will, through a series of clinical vignettes, attempt to capture something of the experience of moving between the paranoid-schizoid and the depressive positions. My examples are offered as illustrations of the ways in which the concepts of the paranoid-schizoid and depressive positions, as interpreted in the previous two chapters,

101

serve to enhance the clinical work of the non-Kleinian therapist.[1]

Before moving to the clinical material, I would like to outline a classification of psychopathology built upon the conceptualizations of the paranoid-schizoid and depressive states of being that were developed in the previous chapters. This conception of levels of psychopathology will serve as a background for the subsequent clinical discussion. (This classification represents a synthesis and extension of the work of Bion [1967], Freud [1896a, 1914, 1915b], Klein [1935, 1975], Fairbairn [1941, 1944, 1946], Kernberg [1970], McDougall [1974], Winnicott [1959–1964], and others.)

The most developmentally advanced group (metaphorically, the "highest level") of psychological disorders reflects conflict in the sphere of personal meanings (including desires) in a personality system that is suffficiently developed for the individual's desires to be experienced as his own. The person is a subject as well as an object who experiences himself as a whole individual, continuous in relation to himself and others over time and space. The person lives in the realm of layered symbolic meanings. Paradigmatic of this level of psychopathology are the neuroses, which are understood in part as manifestations of conflicted oedipal meanings. In the psychopathology of conflicted personal meaning, one's desires—for example, a boy's sexual and filial feelings toward his mother—are experienced as painfully incompatible. Por-

---

[1] I would like to express my gratitude to the therapists whom I have supervised for discussing their clinical work with me in a way that has helped me greatly in developing and clarifying many of the ideas discussed in this chapter.

tions of one's system of meanings are disowned and yet preserved by means of repression and related defenses, e.g., displacement, isolation of affect, intellectualization, and compromise symptom formation. In Kleinian terminology, this is the psychopathology developed in the depressive position.

A second, more primitive group of psychological disturbances involves embattled "impersonal" meanings that are experienced as things in themselves. Desires are not experienced as one's own thoughts and feelings but, rather, as things or forces by which one is attacked, protected, drowned, suffocated, eaten alive, burned, or penetrated. Symbolization is in the form of symbolic equation. Subjectivity is in a rudimentary state of development, and therefore the self is predominantly the self as object that can do things and can be done to but that does not experience itself as the author of desire or the interpreter of experience.

The psychoses are paradigmatic of this form of psychopathology, which is developed in the paranoid-schizoid position. In this schema, a very wide range of psychopathological states (including borderline conditions, pathological narcissism, severe character disorders, psychotic depression, manic-depressive illness, and perversions) are viewed as problems of balance and intercommunication between depressive and paranoid-schizoid modes. In Chapter 8, these "disturbances of balance" will be discussed as the breakdown of a dialectical relationship between reality and phantasy.

A third group of mental disturbances (the "lowest level" of psychopathology) involves the foreclosure of meaning. This is a realm of "nonexperience" in which potential thoughts and feelings are neither attributed symbolic meaning as they are in the neuroses, nor given ex-

istence as things as they are in the psychoses. Examples
of this level of disturbance include psychosomatic illness
(McDougall, 1974), alexithymia (Nemiah, 1977; Sifneos,
1972), and schizophrenic nonexperience (Bion, 1959,
1962a; Ogden, 1981). The person exists but, to the extent
that he has foreclosed meaning, he is psychologically dead.
The psychotic patient has at least generated a psychological illness (albeit one in which feelings and ideas are
treated as things), but even this represents an advance
over a state in which the strain that might have become
experience is for example relegated to the realm of bodily
illness (see McDougall, 1984a). It must be kept in mind
that all three levels of psychopathology are present in
every individual, and therefore that psychosomatic foreclosure of meaning may be a feature to consider in the
treatment of both the neurotic and the psychotic patient.

  With these schema as a rough means for grouping
forms of psychopathology, I turn now to a discussion of
clinical material in which the patient's mode of organizing
experience and mode of object-relatedness shift as the
patient moves between a predominantly paranoid-schizoid
and a predominantly depressive state of being. As will be
discussed, a corresponding shift is required in the therapist's way of listening, his way of conceptualizing the
therapeutic interaction, and his mode of response to the
patient.

Acute Regression to
the Paranoid-Schizoid Position

When a patient is functioning in a predominantly paranoid-schizoid mode, the therapeutic relationship does not
develop in the context of a body of acknowledged, shared
experience. In the extreme, the schizophrenic patient feels

that a new therapist has appeared with each new feeling state (Searles, 1972).

Mr. H., a single man in his early thirties, had suffered since adolescence from intense anxiety of a paranoid type. He had experienced periods of confusion in late adolescence and had been unable to work or attend college. In the course of intensive psychotherapy over a period of seven years, he had been able to graduate from college and handle a responsible job in the computer field. The patient had been born with a congenital heart defect that had alarmed his mother and had led her to "do everything for him, but breathe." Most of his developmental landmarks had been delayed. His father was excluded from the mother–child pair until the patient became school-aged. At that point, the patient's mother abruptly left the patient in the care of his father and a series of housekeepers. Mr. H.'s father made no secret of the fact that he experienced the patient as an "albatross" around his neck.

In the therapy, the patient was very fearful of developing feelings of affection for, or dependence upon, the therapist. Mr. H. continually referred to the therapist as a "necessary evil, like bad-tasting medicine." In the initial years of therapy, Mr. H. led a schizoid existence with practically no real relationships, substituting loud rock music, television, and masturbation for human contact.

I will not focus here on the process by which the patient progressed from his heavy reliance on schizoid withdrawal and communication by means of projective identification to more mature object-relatedness. In the course of this work the patient developed an intense, ambivalent tie to the therapist. As this tie

developed, the patient intermittently experienced homosexual anxiety. At one point, Mr. H. haltingly
mentioned that a friend had commented that one man
can like another man without it being a sign that they
are homosexuals. The patient then said, "It just occurred to me that there must be something like that
going on here, but if you ever remind me that I've
said it, I'll deny it. You know I will."

In the latter part of the seventh year of therapy,
a friend of the patient was in the process of terminat-
ing his therapy, which greatly heightened the patient's anxiety about his feeling of dependence upon
the therapist. At the same time, the patient reported
getting into fights with his boss as a result of what the
patient perceived as the boss's incompetence. Mr. H.
talked at great length about the fact that he didn't
give a damn if his boss tried to fire him because both
he and his boss knew that the patient could get a new
job anytime he wanted.

The therapist, in this period of the work, began
to experience the patient as "sticky," a feeling that
he understood as a reflection of the fear that the
patient might never be able to end this therapy and
that the patient and therapist would "grow old together." The therapist experienced a form of "claustrophobia" when with the patient. Only in retrospect,
after the therapist sought consultation on this case,
did he come to understand this claustrophobia in
terms of a projective identification[2] on the part of the

---

[2]Projective identification, although a primitive mode of defense and
communication, is not exclusively a feature of the paranoid-schizoid
position. Since paranoid-schizoid and depressive modes always coexist, projective identification is a potential facet of all psychological
states and all forms of object-relatedness.

patient, in which feelings congruent with those of the patient's burdened and suffocated (internal object) father and mother were engendered in the therapist. Such feelings led to an intensification of the therapist's then largely unconscious fears of his own inclination (stemming from his own childhood) to cling fearfully to a withdrawing object.

The result of the therapist's inability to manage this projective identification was a series of interventions reflecting the therapist's fearfulness of the patient's (and his own) wishes never to be independent of each other. For example, Mr. H. reported a dream in which the manifest content depicted the patient's chance meeting of a former school teacher whom the patient had greatly admired. In the dream Mr. H. felt proud of all that he had accomplished, but he was afraid that the teacher did not really remember him. He was also afraid that the teacher had not fared well. Only in retrospect did the therapist understand the dream as an expression of the patient's anxiety about completing therapy. This had been represented in the dream by the fear of having been forgotten by the teacher (therapist), and in the anxiety about the welfare of the teacher (therapist) after the separation.

At another point, the therapist drew Mr. H.'s attention to the fact that the patient was now able to manage an aspect of his life that he had been unable to manage earlier. When Mr. H. did finally mention a thought about "someday" finishing therapy, the therapist commented on Mr. H.'s vagueness. The cumulative effect of these and numerous similar interventions was to exacerbate the patient's anxiety about being found to be a destructive drain on the therapist, leading to the therapist's premature termination of the therapy.

Over the weekend following the session in which the therapist had commented on the patient's vagueness with regard to thoughts about termination, Mr. H. become floridly psychotic and was taken to a local emergency room. The therapist was notified and went to meet with the patient. Mr. H. was frightented of the therapist and asked not to be left in a room alone with him. The patient was at times extremely agitated, yelling that the therapist was a dangerous, devious man who had murdered and chopped up dozens of patients and had buried them under his office while pretending to be a "respectable" doctor.

The therapist attempted over a period of hours to talk with the patient. At several points the therapist commented on what had occurred in the last session. He said that he felt that Mr. H. must have felt that the therapist was trying to get rid of the patient when they were discussing the patient's reference to termination. He said that he understood that this must have felt dangerously close to Mr. H.'s experience as a child when he had felt suddenly and absolutely cut off from his mother. The patient kept insisting that he was not going to be manipulated by the therapist's tricks, although he made no effort to leave the room. The therapist made reference to previous events in the therapy that he and the patient had weathered together, but the patient said he considered this just another of the therapist's ploys. The therapist had the fantasy that the person he was talking to in the emergency room was not the same patient with whom he had worked over the previous seven years.

Mr. H. refused to take any medication, nor would he accept from the emergency room staff the names of other therapists whom he might consult. For the next four days, the patient remained in a paranoid state. The therapist was aware that Mr. H. was spending his time in the neighborhood of the therapist's office, but the therapist made no effort either to speak to or to go out of his way to avoid the patient. Neither did he feel afraid of the patient. Beginning on the second of these four days, the patient periodically sat in the therapist's waiting room when he knew that the therapist was not in the building. Mr. H. finally phoned the therapist to ask to resume therapy. In the first of these meetings, the patient seemed to be reacquainting himself with someone whom he had known years before and attempting to determine in what ways the other person had changed. His anger at and distrust of the therapist were present but not overwhelming.

In the months that followed, as the patient became able to reflect upon this period of the therapy, he said that in the emergency room and for most of the week that followed, he had felt certain that the therapist had murdered him and that he was his own ghost who was refusing to die. He had felt that his revenge on the therapist would be to haunt him and he guessed that that was why he felt compelled to spend his time in the therapist's neighborhood. Mr. H. commented again and again that he felt as if he were recounting a dream in remembering this period. The therapist had been like a figure in a nightmare. The cause and effect relationships that he now saw seemed to him to be supplied in retrospect, since at the time he "did not do things for reasons," he did what he did because he "had to." He said he could not really be certain what occurred then and what he was reading into it afterward. In fact, at times he was not sure whether he was making it all up retrospectively; he almost wished he were. Mr. H. said with some amusement that his haunting of the therapist had been a "benign haunting," because he had spent a good deal of his time cleaning up papers from the street.

The therapist told Mr. H. that he understood how his comments had been heard as reflecting the therapist's wish to get rid of Mr. H. and that that must have been terrifying to him. The therapist also said that he felt that the patient had fled as much to protect the therapist from his anger as out of fear of being hurt by him. After all, the patient had symbolically killed and exiled himself and set up a protective vigil for the therapist.

In the period prior to the onset of the psychosis, Mr. H. had attempted to utilize manic defenses, including denial of dependence, devaluation of the object, and omnipotent phantasies of replacing one object by another. In this period, Mr. H.'s boss served as a transference displacement object. When the patient no longer was able to maintain a manic defense, a full-blown regression resulted. Mr. H. then engaged in a radical rewriting of history in his flight from the fears of object loss and destruction of the therapist (a heretofore ambivalently loved object). The therapist was physically recognizable, but was an emotionally different entity, no longer a human being who had shared a body of experience with the patient. Instead, there was a discovery of a new truth that changed everything. The therapist was felt to have been unmasked as an imposter. In this state, the fearfully anticipated loss of the therapist at the end of therapy and the fear of harming the therapist were transformed into a series of assaults and counterassaults between endangered and endangering objects.

In retrospect, the patient's comment that he would deny his affectionate-sexual interest in the therapist if later called upon to acknowledge it, can be heard as a wish that history could be defensively negated. In the depressive position, this disavowal entails an unconscious act of hiding and preserving an aspect of oneself in relation to another person (i.e., repression). In the patient's regression to the paranoid-schizoid position, this disavowal became much more profound and involved a wholesale rewriting of history (based upon splitting), thereby rendering discontinuous the patient and his experience with others. The present was projected backward and forward in time, destroying history as an evolving process and creating a timeless present. Each new affective state was experienced as the discovery of the truth which then discredited previous experience as false illusion.

At this point, I would like to draw attention to two facets of the technical handling of the case. First, in handling the regression to the paranoid-schizoid position, transference interpretation was attempted and its efficacy evaluated. I believe that the interpretation of the meaning of the regression as a response to the patient's fear of abandonment and his wish to retaliate, was accurate. However, since the patient was at that point minimally able to differentiate internal and external reality, his capacity to utilize verbal interpretation was quite limited. The utilization of interpretation involves an act of mediation between symbol and symbolized by a subject who experiences himself as distinct from both. However, even in profound regression, there is almost always an aspect of personality that remains capable of such differentiation (except in full-blown manic and paranoid states). For this reason, interpretation plays a role in the treatment of all phases of regression (see Boyer, 1983; Boyer and Giovacchini, 1967).

Second, the therapist's continued presence during an extended interview, despite the patient's attacks upon him, served a containing function for the patient's psychotic experience. The fact that the patient felt on the verge of disintegration was represented in his delusion of the chopped-up patient buried under the therapist's office. The therapist's nonretaliative attempts to understand the patient's experience offered Mr. H. access to an integrating interaction. The patient did not flee from the room nor did he accept medications or the substitution of another therapist. Instead, he made use of the therapist as a containing presence[3] (both during the interview and later by sitting in the therapist's waiting room and spending his time near the therapist's office) as opposed to using the therapist as an idealized, protective object or as a persecutory object.

Mr. H.'s use of the therapist as a containing presence facilitated his reintegration and return to the therapist as object. At that point the same interpretations were offered that had been made in the emergency room, but because the patient now had more fully reemerged as subject, he could participate in a different way in the process of using symbols to mediate between himself and his immediate lived experience.

---

[3]The idea of a relationship to a containing presence is only hinted at by Klein (1955). This notion was made central by Winnicott and will be discussed in Chapter 7.

A Foray into the Depressive Position

The importance to clinical practice of the recognition of the features of paranoid-schizoid and depressive modes of processing experience is not restricted to the management of dramatic regressions of the type just described. Some patients oscillate between the two psychological organizations in almost every session. However, as in the case that will now be described, forays into a depressive mode may be quite striking when they emerge from a background of long periods of part-object relatedness in which the therapist has hardly ever been acknowledged as a subject.

A therapist had been meeting with Mr. L. early in the morning, before regular hours. This arrangement had become necessary when the patient took a new job. In the two-and-one-half years of these early meetings, Mr. L.'s only acknowledgment of this hour was an occasional complaint about the inconvenience that these appointments had caused him. It therefore came as a surprise to the therapist when the patient said one morning that he felt somewhat embarrassed by his previous blindness to the fact that the therapist also had been inconvenienced by the early appointments. Mr. L. worried that he might be "missing" things that are obvious to other people and that this might put him at a disadvantage socially and in getting ahead at work. The patient had regularly engaged in rather ruthless relations with women and business colleagues. He felt that this was "the way things are done" and rather blithely, guiltlessly, and unapologetically conducted his life in that way.

The therapist did not comment at this point on

the patient's observation about himself. However, the idea that the patient might be "missing" something was over time used by the patient as the hub of a network of ideas to which he would periodically return. The meanings for Mr. L. of the word "missing" became broadened in the course of this work to include not only the idea of failing to perceive something he could use in his "dealings" with others, but also the idea of missing out on a set of feelings that other people feel. This ultimately led to a sense that a part of himself was missing. The fleeting empathy demonstrated by the patient at the point in therapy just described reflected the beginning of a capacity for an awareness of the subjectivity of another person.

The following is another example of the beginning of movement from the paranoid-schizoid to the depressive position, this time reflected in the altered type of reparation the patient attempts in the transference.

Ms. C. regularly expressed her dissatisfaction with the therapy and the therapist but brought the therapist an annual Christmas gift. Even though the patient had been railing at the therapist the previous day, everything was different on the day she brought the gift. There was an air of joviality that was jolting to the therapist even after this had happened for several years. The therapist experienced the gifts as "Trojan horses," angry demands for submission in the guise of a peace offering.

Each time the Christmas gift was given, the therapist interpreted the patient's resistance to considering the meaning of the gift giving. The patient unconsciously viewed these resistance interpretations as indications that the reparative wish had not been recognized or accepted. As a result, the patient would immediately become infuriated and would stubbornly refuse to give any thought at all to the therapist. The therapist was correct that there was a demand being made by the patient that her omnipotent wishes be accepted without modification. However, the therapist's failure to recognize and acknowledge the fact that the wish was in part reparative led the patient to defensively withdraw the gesture and substitute raw hostility.

In the fourth year of therapy, the therapist was suddenly called away for two weeks because of the death of a relative. This was the only time that the therapist had had to cancel Ms. C.'s therapy hours on short notice. The therapist phoned the patient and told her that something unexpected had occurred and that she would be away for two weeks. When the therapist returned, Ms. C. brought some food that she had baked. The food itself was not the gift. The gift was the patient's willingness to attempt to talk about the meaning of the present. Formerly, the gift itself had the magical function of makings things right, clearing the air, and creating good feeling. Now the patient seemed to sense that the object given was inert and that her effort to express reparative concern for the therapist must be located in an intersubjective process of offering something of herself to the therapist as a separate person with her own subjectivity.

Earlier in the therapy, this patient could not

have empathized sufficiently with the therapist to
have known what the therapist might have wanted.
The therapist had been treated almost entirely as an
externalization of one or more of the patient's internal objects. In the giving of the gift following the
therapist's absence, the patient seemed to have genuinely given something to the therapist, something
that she had created (food that she had cooked and
thoughts that she had thought) and therefore, symbolically, had given something of herself. Also, one
might speculate that the gift of food had particular
empathic significance in that it might have reflected
the patient's conscious or unconscious suspicion that
a death had occurred and that the therapist might be
comforted by food, as in the oral symbolism manifested in a wake.

On the occasion of the patient's giving of the
food and the attendant associations, the therapist
simply thanked the patient and did not interpret resistance to further associations. This resulted in the
patient's feeling that her wish to make up for what
she had done (and thought) had been accepted by the
therapist. The shared experience could be and was
discussed later. When subsequent gifts were offered,
the therapist did not immediately interpret the associated resistances. The earlier interpretation of resistance represented a disguised counterattack on the
part of the therapist and therefore was itself a part of
a transference-countertransference acting out.

It is unfortunate when a therapist feels obligated
to interpret immediately either the expressive or the
resistant facet of transference acting out or acting in.
It may take months or years before this can be done

in a productive way, but that delay does not necessarily mean that one is involved in a therapy that attempts only to be a corrective emotional experience.

The Creation of Psychic Reality

A different mode of analytic work becomes possible as the space between symbol and symbolized is created in the course of therapy. The capacity to make this differentiation enables the patient to view his thoughts, feelings, perceptions, and behavior as constructions, as opposed to impersonal registrations of fact. Only when one's behavior is viewed (at least in part) as a personal symbolic construction can one be curious about why one does what one does, how one does it, with whom one does it, and when one does it.

A bulimic patient became aware for the first time after a year of therapy that there was an irony in the fact that she came to therapy at a great "sacrifice" of time, money, and effort in order to rid herself of her bulimia, and yet carefully arranged to have time to "binge" after each therapy hour. Earlier in the therapy, she simply had done these things and had never consciously thought about it. With the psychological shift reflected in the awareness of the irony involved in her behavior, it became possible to utilize the patient's repeated references to the potential power of her aggressiveness, demandingness and controllingness to help her understand the way in which devouring food after the meetings had served in the patient's (unconscious) mind to protect the therapist from being eaten alive by the patient. What had been something happening to the patient (a need to binge) became her wish (to eat in a particular way) that served to deflect dangerous feelings from the therapist and thereby safeguard the relationship with the therapist.

Freud's (1932) statement of the analytic goal, "Where it was, there I shall be (or shall be becoming)" ("*Wo Es war, soll Ich werden*")[4], is an eloquent description of the experiential shift involved in the movement from a paranoid-schizoid to a depressive state. In this light, the goal of psychoanalysis is the transformation of that which had been an impersonal event (it) that is happening to me (e.g., an anxiety "attack," a "wave" of depression, an irresistible "need" to binge, to take drugs, to put oneself in physical danger), into an experience that has a quality of "I-ness." For example, a compulsion to starve myself that has been an irresistible urgent need may come to be experienced as something I am doing, and doing in a particular way because I am convinced (for reasons that I may come to understand) that if I starve myself, I will not be accused or accuse myself of being greedy, or perverse, or murderous. Oral deprivation is an expression of my belief that eating will result in my having a body of a feared weight, shape, size, texture, or odor, all of which are shameful signs of what I have done, the way I have

---

[4]This statement was mistranslated by Strachey as "Where id was, there ego shall be" (Freud, 1932, p. 80). Freud (1926) explicitly cautioned against the use of "orotund Greek names" (p. 195) for the labeling of these everyday experiences of self and of inanimate nonself (within ourselves).

done it, and the reasons for which I have done it. In the process of "it" becoming "me," it becomes possible for me to understand why I hold so tightly to this conviction, how I developed the conviction, and the nature of the pain that I would feel in relinquishing it.

Oedipal-Level Transference and Countertransference

Often when a patient has begun to enter a realm of experience that is predominantly of a depressive quality, oedipal content emerges in the transference and countertransference. The feelings involved in the oedipal situation, e.g., ambivalent triangular object ties, guilt, jealousy, and rivalry are reflections of the fact that the development of the capacity for whole object-relatedness is well under way. There are primitive precursors of such experience in the paranoid-schizoid position, e.g., envy of the possessions of the object. However, the quality of experience in the paraniod-schizoid position is quite different from the oedipal situation developed in the depressive position. For example, the anxiety and guilt involved in wishing to defeat and murder the same person one loves is an entirely different experience from that of wishing to destroy or steal valued (envied) contents of a split-off bad object.

A therapist had been seeing Ms. D. in intensive psychotherapy for about five years. The therapy had been a productive one, and the patient, who had initially been diagnosed as schizophrenic, had begun to relate and function in increasingly mature ways. The analytic work had centered around the patient's fears of melting into, taking over, or being taken over by the therapist. Ms. D. had gone through periods of intense rage toward the therapist, some of which were experienced in the form of shrieking in the sessions. A great deal of the anger, however, was displaced onto Ms. D.'s husband, with whom the patient engaged in violent physical fights. Primitive sexual feelings were disguised as, and confused with, anger in these fights. There also had been long periods over the course of this therapy in which Ms. D. had fearfully withdrawn from the therapist and had sat silently during many of these meetings.

The consuming intensity of the transference feelings was understood and interpreted as a repetition of aspects of the patient's relationship with her mother. Ms. D.'s mother, a chronically depressed woman, relied heavily upon the patient as a receptacle into which to dump her misery. She would also periodically fly into rages at the patient. In the course of therapy, Ms. D. came to understand her role in unconsciously provoking her mother's rages as a way of consolidating the bond with her mother when she became anxious that her mother was "drifting away."

In the fifth year of therapy, the therapist began to be aware that, although he had enjoyed working with this patient, he was now for the first time finding the patient sexually attractive. During this period, Ms. D. reported no dreams (in sharp contrast to the previous abundance of dream material) and seemed to be coyly secretive as opposed to being angrily or fearfully withdrawn.

In the initial years of therapy, the patient had felt painfully weak and inadequate in comparison to the therapist and her husband, both of whom she idealized as powerful, protective men. The patient had derived no pleasure from either foreplay or sexual intercourse with her husband, but did enjoy the cuddling that preceded and followed sex.

In the period that followed the therapist's initial awareness of the patient's sexual attractiveness, the patient's attitude toward sex shifted dramatically. She began to complain that her husband was clumsy and insensitive sexually. She had fantasies during intercourse with her husband of having sex with other men. Ms. D. began seriously to consider leaving her husband. During this period the patient experienced intense anxiety when in the presence of any man, including the therapist. She felt that the anxiety derived from a fear of being seen to have sexual thoughts and feelings. She imagined that she would feel humiliated if anyone knew that she had sexual feelings, even though she intellectually knew that such feelings were universal. Eventually the patient began to realize that it was her wish for a sexual relationship with the therapist that would be the most humiliating revelation. She felt that it would be humiliating in large part because it would be unreciprocated and that she would feel like a pathetic fool.

The patient, to this point in therapy, had said extremely little about her father, but during this period she discussed what she had been told about her father's desertion of the family when she was just under 2 years of age. The father had remarried and maintained contact with the patient in an unpredictable way throughout her childhood and adult life. Her relationship with him was characterized by an idealization of his new family, from which the patient felt painfully excluded. The patient connected her fear of being a fool in relation to the therapist with her feeling that her affection toward her father had been either unrecognized or unvalued.

This work had the familiar ring of the beginning of the analysis of whole-object-related oedipal transference feelings. However, an analysis of the material exclusively at this level would have been incomplete. There was a form of enactment that surrounded this self-reflective analytic work that communicated another level of meaning. This phase of the work was continually punctuated by crises. For example, Ms. D. would call the therapist in the late evening choking on her tears, saying that she was feeling unable to breathe because of intense anxiety about going off alone to work the following day. She was behind in her work and felt completely "unprepared" to face it again. The therapist in this instance told the patient that he felt that she must have felt unprepared for the feelings that she had had during the session that day and that she was afraid she could not manage those feelings on her own until the next meeting.

In the next meeting two days later, Ms. D. said that she had felt annoyed at the therapist for asking her to do something (i.e., think about what had happened in the meeting), when her intention in calling him was to get him to do something for her. However, at the same time, she noticed that her anger had served as a distraction from, and therefore as a relief from, the anxiety and fear that she had been feeling. In the course of their phone conversation, she could feel herself breathing more easily. She said that the more she thought about it, the more she wondered whether the therapist had intended this effect. She was aware that if this were so, she would again be falling into an intense dependence upon the therapist and she did not want to feel that this was the case. The therapist noted, but did not interpret to the patient, that she had defensively transformed her disappointment and annoyance into magical idealization.

Crises during this period of the therapy could be understood as reflections of anxiety generated in the face of conflicted transference feelings, predominantly of an oedipal nature. Enacted in the crises was a flight from whole-object relations by means of a re-creation of unmediated sensory closeness that is involved in primitive object-relatedness characteristic of the paranoid-schizoid position. In a predominantly depressive mode, ideas, feelings, and dreams are placed in the analytic space between patient and therapist for both to reflect upon and to experience.

In contrast, crises are not events that stand between separate people. They are events in which the patient and therapist are "in it together." At one point in a crisis the patient asked the therapist, "What are *we* going to do?" Crises were an effort to reestablish an unmediated sensory closeness; the patient desperately missed such closeness while functioning in a mature mode of relatedness involving intimacy mediated by the separateness of subjects using symbols for communication and for self-reflection. The inevitable isolation of whole-object relatedness (the anxiety of going off alone to work or of managing feelings alone between sessions) was part of what the patient felt "unprepared for."

Thus, this phase of Ms. D.'s psychotherapy was characterized by advances in the development of the depressive mode, including the elaboration of whole-object-related oedipal transferences and countertransferences.

Defensive regression to the paranoid-schizoid mode was motivated by a flight from conflicted personal oedipal meanings and a flight from the inevitable distance/isolation encountered in the symbolically mediated quality of experience in the depressive position.

The Oedipus complex facilitates the triangularization of experience. Lacan (1957, 1961; see also Lemaire, 1970) has discussed the way in which the name-of-the-father as carrier of symbols and names serves as the essential intermediary between mother and infant. Without the thirdness introduced by the child's unconscious identification with the father, and without the system of symbols provided by language, the infant would never be able to distance himself from his mother or from his own experience sufficiently to engage in mediated (self-reflective) experience.

The following clinical material, taken from the psychotherapy of a seriously disturbed, borderline woman, provides a second illustration of the role of the oedipal configuration in the process of individuation in the depressive position.

Ms. N., a 27-year-old college student, had been bulimic for five years prior to the beginning of therapy, which had commenced when she was 21 years old. The bulimia continued through the first four years of therapy, at which point the patient entered into an erotized romantic relationship with a college professor about thirty years her senior. The relationship, which was in its second year at the time being focused upon here, was never explicitly sexual. The following excerpt is taken from a session in the fifth year of therapy.

The patient began the session by telling the therapist that a great deal had happened since they had last met two days earlier and that the therapist should just sit back and listen. The patient told the therapist that during the previous day she had been studying in the park and had talked with a very handsome man a few years older than she. Ms. N. wondered whether the therapist was jealous of the interest being shown in the patient and even suspected she might be trying to make the therapist jealous.

Before class, on the morning of this session, Ms. N. had chatted with the teacher with whom she was infatuated. She had told him about the man in the park, but had exaggerated her involvement with him. Later in the conversation, she coquettishly had asked him if he would "give her away" in the wedding if she married the man in the park. He had said, "Yes, but reluctantly."

The teacher was at the time organizing an academic committee and asked the patient along with several other students to participate in it. The patient offered an excuse for not becoming a member of the committee even though she felt she would very much like to have done so. She felt she could not participate because the committee was to meet at a time that she regularly set aside for her elaborate rituals that preceded her bingeing and vomiting episodes. Ms. N. then cried and beseeched the therapist not to attempt to get her to give up her bingeing and vomiting because she did not feel she could live without it.

Ms. N. had begun this meeting by asking that the therapist not interfere while the patient played with romantic oedipal daydreams in the therapist's presence. The patient was in part aware of her efforts to make the therapist/mother jealous, but was unaware that she was attempting to secure the permission of the therapist to be interested in anyone other than the therapist. (Symbolically, the patient was asking for her mother's blessing for her wish to engage in an oedipal romance with her father.)

The professor with whom the patient was flirting intuitively took the role of a devoted father in the throes of a romance with his daughter, a romance that he knows, and in part regrets, must not become overtly sexual and which must end by his being replaced by another man. The patient coyly teased the teacher with stories about a younger man, to which the professor jealously responded with an invitation of his own. The professor's acting out of the patient's phantasy was in part gratifying and in part frightening to the patient.

The romance with a transference father served as an essential wedge between the mother/therapist and daughter/patient. The emotional presence of the father introduced thirdness, a vantage point outside of the mother–infant dyad. This thirdness offered the possibility of a perspective from which the daughter might (by identification) view herself and her relationship with her mother. In this sense, the Oedipus complex is the exit from the nonreflective, twoness of the paranoid-schizoid position. However, Ms. N. was deeply divided about making use of this exit. In effect, she told herself and her transference father (the professor) that her loyalty to her internal object mother came first. She was not willing or able to give up the tie to the internal object mother (represented in the bulimic symptomatology) sufficiently to make room for a third. This primitive tie to the internal object-mother is not at all comparable to the tie to the father or mother in the oedipal situation. The mother of bingeing and vomiting is a mother of bodily functions who is inseparable from oneself, whom one devours, mixes with one's blood, and then partially vomits out in order not to disappear into her or be taken over by her. This is the mother to whom the patient is conflictedly loyal, enslaved, and enmeshed. The therapist as oedipal object-mother threatens to interfere with a more primitive tie to the internal object-mother related to in the act of bingeing and vomiting, and formerly related to in the symbiotic transference to the therapist. The patient begged the oedipal object-mother/therapist not to insist that she give up the tie to the more primitive, internal object-mother.

The introduction by the patient of romantic/sexual feelings for the teacher reflected the introduction of thirdness, both in the realm of object relations and in the arena of symbol formation. Ms. N. at the same time as she developed a "crush" on her teacher, became curious about the meanings of experience (e.g., her bingeing). The patient, as interpreting subject, could serve as a third entity interposed between symbol and symbolized, i.e., between her thoughts (her symbolic constructions) and that which she was thinking about (the symbolized).

As in the case of Ms. D. described earlier, the patient was deeply torn by the prospect of the introduction of thirdness. Thirdness offered relief from the feeling of painful entrapment in the dependence upon the therapist; at the same time, there was an intense sense of loss involved in giving up the feeling of unmediated relatedness that had been experienced in the more primitive relationship to the mother/therapist. The pain involved in the renunciation of this (phantasied) life-sustaining form

of relatedness is a significant part of what is depressive
about the "depressive" position.

The Creation of Reflective Distance

Still another clinical feature of the entry into the depressive position is the sense of development of reflective
distance from oneself, in which "I" can observe "me." A
patient described her experience prior to this development
as a "flurry of activity":

> A friend who had not seen me for about a year told
> me that until today he felt that when he looked into
> my eyes he could see right through me. I know what
> he means. What you saw was what you got. He was
> not intending to be insulting. I used to strike him as
> honest and straightforward and he liked that. He's
> not so sure he likes me being more mysterious, maybe
> even deceptive.
>
> It's not as if I'm off in the corner observing
> myself. The awareness of myself and the doing are in
> the same place. I can feel the wind against the backs
> of my calves when I walk. It's not that I never used to
> think about myself or be self-reflective, but this is
> different.
>
> There is me and there is something inside me,
> not something, but someone, but since that someone
> is inside me, I can have some idea who it is and not
> just be it. Sometimes this is connected with a feeling
> that it's a physical space inside my body, but it's
> sometimes in my head or isn't located any specific
> place in my body. It's a feeling, not a place, but it
> feels like a place.

Concluding Comments

These clinical accounts have been offered in an attempt to provide a sense of the way in which a conceptualization of paranoid-schizoid and depressive modes of experience may serve to help the therapist organize clinical data. The use of these ideas, it is hoped, will facilitate empathy with "the it" while the therapist facilitates the patient's efforts to more fully become a subject.

―――― 6 ――――
Internal Object Relations

Object relations theory, often erroneously thought to be an exclusively interpersonal theory that diverts attention from the unconscious, is in fact fundamentally a theory of unconscious internal[1] object relations in dynamic interplay with current interpersonal experience. The analysis of internal object relations centers upon the exploration of the relationship between internal objects and the ways in which the patient resists altering these unconscious internal object relations in the face of current experience. Classical theory does not include a concept of internal objects. Instead there are related and, in part, overlapping concepts of memory traces, mental representations of self and object, introjects, identifications, and psychic structures.

It is the thesis of this chapter that the "internalization" of an object relationship necessarily involves a split-

[1]In this chapter, the term "internal" will be used to refer not to a geographic locale, but to an intrapersonal event (i.e., an event involving a single personality system) as opposed to an interpersonal interaction involving two or more people.

131

ting of the ego[2] into parts that, when repressed, constitute internal objects which stand in a particular unconscious relationship to one another. This internal relationship is shaped by the nature of the original object relationship but does not by any means bear a one-to-one correspondence to it, and is potentially modifiable by subsequent experience. The internal object relationship may be later reexternalized by means of projection and projective identification in an interpersonal setting, thus generating the transference and countertransference phenomena of analysis and all other interpersonal interactions.

I further propose that internal objects be thought of as dynamically unconscious suborganizations of the ego capable of generating meaning and experience, i.e., capable of thought, feeling, and perception. These suborganizations stand in unconscious relationships to one another and include (1) self-suborganizations of ego, i.e., aspects of the ego in which the person more fully experiences his ideas and feelings as his own, and (2) object suborganizations of ego, through which meanings are generated in a mode based upon an identification of an aspect of the ego with the object. This identification with the object is so thorough that one's original sense of self is almost entirely lost. This conception of internal object relations goes well beyond the classical notion of self and object mental representations (see Hartmann, 1964; Jacobson, 1964;

---

[2]The term *ego* will be used to refer to an aspect of personality capable of generating conscious and unconscious psychological meanings including perceptual meanings, cognitive meanings, and emotional meanings. As development proceeds, this aspect of personality becomes increasingly capable not only of organizing and linking individual meanings in the process of thinking, remembering, loving, hating, etc., but also of regulating the relationship between suborganizations of ego that have been split off from the original whole.

Sandler and Rosenblatt, 1962). Proposed here is the idea that the ego is split into parts, each capable of generating experience in a mode modeled after either one's sense of an object in an early object relationship experience or one's experience of oneself in the same early object relationship. The two parts of the ego remain linked and, when repressed, constitute an unconscious internal object relationship.

This conceptualization of internal object relations is an outgrowth of the work of Freud, Abraham, Melanie Klein, Fairbairn, Winnicott, and Bion. Although there are significant theoretical differences among this group of analysts, the concept of internal objects has been handled by each of them in such a way as to lay the groundwork for the next, in what together constitutes a central line of thought of object relations theory. The contribution of each of these analysts to the concept of internal object relationships will be discussed, and an integrated conception of the nature of internal object relations will be presented. I will then show how the clinical phenomena of transference, countertransference, and resistance can be understood more fully when viewed from the perspective of the theory of internal objects proposed.

An Object Relations Theory of Internal Objects

Freud

Freud did not use the term "internal objects," nor did he generate a conceptualization equivalent to that which will be discussed as an object relations conception of internal objects. In *The Interpretation of Dreams* (1900), Freud implied that unconscious memory traces had the power to perpetuate the feelings involved in forgotten early experience, could attract attention to themselves in the course of dream and symptom formation, and could press for conscious expression, dream representation, and symbolic representation in symptomatic behavior and character pathology. In 1914, Freud introduced the idea that unconscious phantasies about objects may under certain circumstances take the place of actual relationships with people.

In "Mourning and Melancholia" (1917), identification is viewed as the means by which one not only remembers, but in part emotionally replaces, a lost external object with an aspect of oneself that has been modeled after the lost external object. Freud described how in melancholia a relationship with an external object is "transformed . . . into a cleavage between the critical activity of the ego and the ego as altered by identification" (p. 249). In other words, an external relationship is replaced by an internal one that involves an interplay of two *active* aspects of the person that have resulted from a splitting of the ego.

In 1923, Freud extended the notion of identification to include not only a modeling of oneself after the external object, but, as in the case of superego formation, a process by which the functions of the external object are instated within the psyche. Freud (1940a) at the end of his life summarized his theory of structure formation by which a new active agency is generated:

> A portion of the external world has, at least partially, been abandoned as an object and has instead, by identification, been taken into the ego and thus become an integral part of the internal world. This new psychical agency continues to carry on the functions

which have hitherto been performed by the people [the abandoned objects] in the external world: it observes the ego, gives it orders, judges it and threatens it with punishments, exactly like parents whose place it has taken. (p. 205)

Freud thus proposes a model wherein an external object is "by identification . . . taken into the ego." He goes on to explain that taking the object into the ego involves establishing "a new psychical agency," i.e., an aspect of personality that has the capacity to carry on functions in the internal world previously performed in the external world by the object. This new agency stands in relation to the ego and can perceive, think, respond, and initiate activity. Further, it has its own system of motivations: "it observes the ego, gives it orders, judges it and threatens it with punishments." Freud is here describing a normal developmental sequence wherein the child, in the context of his relations with external objects, establishes a suborganization of ego that has the capacity for independent motivation and carries on an object relationship with other aspects of the ego.

Freud's "Fetishism" (1927) and "Splitting of the Ego in the Process of Defense" (1940b) invoke the concept of a split in the ego[3] to account for the way in which one can know and not know at the same time. In other words, the ego can be defensively divided so as to operate on the basis of different types of understanding of reality. This repre-

---

[3]Bettelheim (1983) pointed out that "the ego" is an incorrect translation of "*das Ich*" which is more accurately translated as "the I." The phrase "splitting of the I" better captures the notion of a subdivision of the person's capacity to think, perceive, and create experience than does the more impersonal "splitting of the ego."

sents both a clarification of the process of ego splitting involved in superego formation and an extension of the idea to account for internal division within the personality, other than that involved in superego formation.

Abraham

Freud's concept of psychic structures or "agencies" operating in an "internal world" that is developed in the context of one's early relations with external objects constitutes the theoretical framework within which all succeeding contributions to object relations theory were developed. Karl Abraham's work played a pivotal role in the development of the object relations branch of psychoanalytic theory and in particular provided the foundation upon which both Klein and Fairbairn developed their ideas. Working within the framework of Freud's sexual instinct theory, Abraham (1924) placed more importance than did Freud on the role of the object in libidinal development and placed more emphasis on the place of unconscious phantasy in psychological life. Abraham's division of early development into preambivalent, ambivalent, and postambivalent phases was the forerunner of Klein's and Fairbairn's schizoid[4] and depressive levels of early psychological organization. Inherent in Abraham's conception of different forms of ambivalence toward objects was the notion that a variety of forms of psychological conflict existed over the experience of self-object differentiation.

[4]Klein initially used the term *paranoid position* but, under the influence of Fairbairn's work, adopted the term *paranoid-schizoid position* in 1952 (Klein, 1975, p. 2n).

Klein

While Abraham's contributions to object relations theory consisted largely in his shift of emphasis within the conceptual framework provided by Freud, Melanie Klein (1975), by making the role of unconscious internal object relationships primary, introduced a new perspective from which to organize clinical and metapsychological thinking. Klein (1946, 1958) conceived of the infant at birth as functioning with a primitive, loosely organized, but whole ego in relation to an object that is experienced as whole. Under the pressure of the intolerable anxiety of impending annihilation produced by the death instinct, the infant defensively attempts to distance himself from his sense of destructiveness by splitting both the ego and the object into more manageable (because separate) good and bad facets of object-related experience. Stated in less mechanical terms, the infant simplifies an unmanageably complicated relationship with the mother (including the coexistence of hating and loving feelings felt toward and experienced from the mother) by treating the relationship as if it were many relationships between unmistakably loving and unmistakably malevolent conceptions of self and object. These aspects of the infant's relationship with the object are kept separate by means of projective and introjective phantasies. The infant's splitting of his experience of his relationships with objects allows him to create a psychological sanctuary (safe from hostile and destructive feelings) within which he can feed safely, take in safely what he needs from his mother.

This theory of early development established a conception of psychological life based upon an internal organization derived from the relationship of split-off aspects

of the ego to associated internal objects. There are considerable shortcomings in Klein's theory of internal object
relations. Most fundamentally, Klein is not clear whether
she views internal object relations as phantasies or as
relationships between active agencies capable of feeling,
thinking, and perceiving. In fact, she says both and often
mixes the two by formulating clinical phenomena in terms
of relationships between an active agency and a thought
(see Mackay, 1981). This involves a confusion of levels of
abstraction analogous to saying that a thought is contained in a neuron.

The fallacy of establishing direct relations between
active agencies and ideas permeates Klein's writing. For
example, in describing the development of early psychological life, Klein writes, "The splitting off of persecutory
figures which go to form part of the unconscious is bound
up with splitting off idealized figures as well. Idealized
figures are developed to protect the ego against the terrifying ones" (1958, p. 241). Classical analysts point out that
the notion of idealized figures protecting the ego against
terrifying ones is tantamount to proposing that there are
internal friendly and hostile "demons" operating within
the mind. "A multitude of minds is introduced into a
single psychic apparatus . . . the person is being envisaged
as a container of innumerable, independent microorgani-
zations that are also microdynamisms" (Schafer, 1968,
p. 62). Kleinians have replied that these figures are not
demons but, rather, unconscious phantasies: "Internal
objects are not 'objects' situated in the body or the
psyche: like Freud [in his theory of the superego] Melanie
Klein is describing unconscious phantasies which people
have about what they contain" (Segal, 1964, p. 12). Despite this clarification on the part of the Kleinians, however, it must be remembered that an unconscious phan-

tasy (the product of "phantasy-thinking" [Isaacs, 1952, p. 108]) is, after all, a thought, as are the figures within the phantasy. If internal objects are thoughts, as Segal and Isaacs conceptualize them to be, then they cannot themselves think, perceive, or feel, nor can they protect or attack the ego. Even to the present, Kleinian theorists have not been able to disentangle themselves from the Scylla of demonology and the Charybdis of mixing incompatible levels of abstraction (i.e., active agencies and thoughts).

Fairbairn

This Kleinian theory of internal object relations, with its unsatisfactory mixture of phantasy and dynamism, together with Freud's theory of the origin of the superego, formed the background for Fairbairn's contributions to object relations theory. Fairbairn (1940, 1944), like Klein, viewed the infantile ego as whole at birth and capable of relating to whole external objects. To the extent that the "fit" between mother and infant is lacking, the infant experiences an intolerable feeling of disconnectedness and defends himself by means of splitting off the aspects of the ego which were felt to be unacceptable to the mother. These split-off portions of ego remain fixed in a relationship with the unsatisfactory aspect of the object. This part-object relationship (split-off ego in relation to an emotionally absent or rejecting object) is repressed in order to master the feelings involved and in an effort to change the object into a satisfactory object. The ego and frustrating object undergo further subdivisions along lines of cleavage determined by different affective qualities of the unsatisfactory object relationship. For example, the tantalizing qualities of the relationship and the rejecting qualities of the relationship become separated from one another in the infant's internal world. A significant aspect of the ego (the central ego) retains a relationship with the accepting and accepted qualities of the object (the "good enough" mother [Winnicott, 1951] as opposed to the defensively idealized mother). The central ego is in part the conscious ego but also includes dynamically unconscious facets, e.g., its defensive efforts to make itself unaware of the unsatisfactory aspects of object-related experience.

Fairbairn, although working within a Freudian psychoanalytic framework, was struggling against what he felt were shortcomings of both the Freudian and the Kleinian theories. Fairbairn (1946) pointed out that Freud (1932) conceived of the id as energy without structure and the ego as structure without energy; the id was seen as "instinctual cathexes seeking discharge—that in our view is all there is in the id" (Freud, 1932, p. 74), and the ego was perceived as organized into functions but lacking its own source of energy. Fairbairn (1944, 1946) replaced the Freudian dichotomy of ego and id, structure and energy, with a notion of "dynamic structures." These dynamic structures are conceived of as aspects of the mind capable of acting as independent agencies with their own motivational systems. In psychological terms, Fairbairn is saying that these aspects of the person have the capacity to think and to wish according to their own system of generating meaning. According to this theory, each bit of ego (aspect of the personality) defensively split off in the course of development functions as an entity in relation to internal objects and in relation to other subdivisions of the ego.

With regard to the important question of the theoretical status of internal objects, Fairbairn states:

In the interest of consistency, I must now draw the logical conclusion of my theory of dynamic structure and acknowledge that, since internal objects are structures, they must necessarily be, in some measure at least, dynamic. In drawing this conclusion and making this acknowledgment, I shall not only be here following the precedent of Freud, but also, it would seem, conforming to the demands of such psychological facts as are revealed, e.g., in dreams and in the phenomena of paranoia. . . . It must be recognized, however, that, in practice, it is very difficult to differentiate between the activity of internalized objects and the activity of the ego structures with which they are associated; and, with a view to avoiding any appearance of demonology, it seems wise to err, if anything, on the side of overweighting the activity of the ego structures rather than otherwise. It remains true, nevertheless, that under certain conditions internalized objects may acquire a dynamic independence which cannot be ignored. It is doubtless in this direction that we must look for an explanation of the fundamental animism of human beings, which is nonetheless persistent under the surface. . . . (1944, p. 132)

Fairbairn's conclusion that not only ego suborganizations, but also internal objects, must be considered "in some measure at least" to be dynamic structures, fully establishes the concept of internal object relations between active semiautonomous agencies within a single personality. However, the passage just quoted demonstrates that Fairbairn hesitated in drawing his conclusion. In large part it seemed overly close to Klein's formulations, which he considered demonologic. There are a number of incompletely formulated aspects of Fairbairn's theory which may have contributed to his misgivings about this facet of his thinking.

In studying Fairbairn's work, one searches in vain for definitions of the terms *structure* and *dynamic*. (One also is unable to find a definition of the concept of psychic structure in Freud's writing.) I infer from Fairbairn's use of the term *structure* that he is thinking of a stable set of ideas or mental representations. These conscious and unconscious ideas are consistent beliefs in terms of which one plans and measures one's behavior and one's responses to new experience. But these ideas do not themselves think, respond, or perceive. The capacity for thinking, feeling, and perceiving is the basis for the determination that an aspect of the personality is dynamic.

When Fairbairn says that internal objects are not "mere objects" but dynamic structures, he seems to mean that internal figures are not simply mental representations of objects but, rather, active agencies whose activity is perceived by themselves and by other dynamic structures to have specific characteristics, which are then organized and registered as stable mental representations. Structure may exist without dynamism (stable sets of ideas or convictions), but it is not possible for there to be dynamism without structure. For Fairbairn, the concept of id as energy reservoir is replaced by a notion of an unconscious set of ego and object structures, each capable of psychological activity of varying degrees of primitivity.

It remains unclear in Fairbairn's thinking what relationship the concept of ego bears to the concept of dynamic internal objects. Can there be dynamic structure (e.g., an internal object) that is distinct from ego? This appears to be what Fairbairn is saying and, as will be discussed later, may be the reason for his hesitancy to acknowledge fully the dynamic nature of internal objects.

Winnicott

Donald Winnicott's major contribution to the theory of internal object relations is the concept of multiple self-organizations functioning in relation to one another within the personality system. Winnicott (1951, 1952, 1954, 1960a) envisioned the infant as born with the potential for unique individuality of personality (termed a True Self personality organization), which can develop in the context of a responsive holding environment provided by a good-enough mother. However, when a mother substitutes something of herself for the infant's spontaneous gesture (e.g., her own anxiety over separateness for the infant's curious exploration), the infant experiences traumatic disruption of his developing sense of self. When such "impingements" are a central feature of the early mother–child relationship, the infant will attempt to defend himself by developing a second (reactive) personality organization (the False Self organization). This False Self vigilantly monitors and adapts to the conscious and unconscious needs of the mother and in so doing provides a protective exterior behind which the True Self is afforded the privacy that it requires to maintain its integrity.

The False Self is not conceived of as malevolent. On the contrary, the caretaker self (1954) energetically "manages" life so that an inner self might not experience the threat of annihilation resulting from excessive pressure to develop according to the internal logic of another person (e.g., the mother). The dread of annihilation experienced by the True Self results in a feeling of utter dependence on the False Self personality organization. This makes it extremely difficult for a person to diminish his reliance on this False Self mode of functioning despite an awareness of the emptiness of life that devolves from such functioning. Functioning in this mode can frequently lead to academic, vocational, and social success, but over time the person increasingly experiences himself as bored, "going through the motions," detached, mechanical, and lacking spontaneity (see Ogden, 1976).

The theoretical status of the object is not discussed by Winnicott, but his writing makes it clear that he treats internal objects as mental representations. Both Fairbairn's theory of dynamic structure and Winnicott's conception of the True and False Selves represent steps in the development of an object relations theory in which unconscious aspects of the person, each with the capacity to generate meanings according to its own patterns of linkage, engage in internal relationships with one another. Implicit in Fairbairn's and Winnicott's thinking is the idea that conceptualizing intrapsychic conflict as an unconscious phantasy of opposing internal forces does not adequately capture the way in which the person is in fact feeling, thinking, perceiving, and behaving in two ways at once, not simply imagining that to be the case. According to Fairbairn and Winnicott, it is more accurate to say that the person is behaving as two people at once than to say he is thinking about being two people at odds with each other.

Bion

With the unsettled issue of the theoretical status of internal objects in mind, a consideration of aspects of the work of Wilfred Bion becomes particularly pertinent. Bion at first described projective identification as an interpersonal process in which one finds oneself "being manipulated so as to be playing a part, no matter how difficult to recognize, in somebody else's phantasy" (1952, p. 149). In the interpersonal setting, the person projectively identifying engages in an unconscious phantasy of ejecting an unwanted or endangered aspect of himself and of depositing that part in another person in a controlling way. Interpersonal pressure is exerted on the "recipient" of the projective identification, pressure that is unconsciously designed to coerce the "recipient" into experiencing himself and behaving in a way that is congruent with the unconscious projective phantasy. Under optimal circumstances, the recipient "contains" (Bion, 1962a) or "processes" (i.e., handles maturely) the evoked feelings and ideas, and thus makes available for reinternalization by the projector, a more manageable and integrable version of that which had been projected. (See Ogden, 1979, 1981, 1982a for more detailed discussions of projective identification.)

Bion (1957) later made clear that he viewed projective identification not only as an interpersonal process but as an intrapersonal process as well. He conceives of the individual as composed of multiple personality suborganizations, each capable of functioning semiautonomously, and thus capable of processing one another's projective identifications. As can be seen from the foregoing discussion, this view of the personality system is an outgrowth of Klein's, Fairbairn's, and Winnicott's contributions to object relations theory.

For Bion (1956, 1957) projective identification involves the splitting of the personality (not simply a splitting of self-representations) and an ejection of the resulting suborganization into an internal object. The schizophrenic, because of an almost complete incapacity to tolerate reality, replaces perception with an extreme

form of projective identification. By fragmenting perceptual functions into isolated component parts and then
projecting these functions (still experienced to some extent as self) into the object, the schizophrenic creates a
type of internal object termed a "bizarre object." The
object is then experienced as having life of its own: "In
the patient's phantasy the expelled particles of ego lead an
independent and uncontrollable existence outside the personality, but either containing or contained by external
objects" (1956, p. 39). An example given by Bion is the
projection of the visual function into a gramophone (more
accurately, the psychological representation of the gramophone), thus producing a bizarre object felt to be capable
of spying upon the patient. It is as if a part of the personality "has become a thing" (1957, p. 48). This type of defensive fragmentation and projection of the mind into an
object (representation) is the hallmark of the psychotic
personality.

Bion stresses the role of phantasy in the process of
generating bizarre objects. In so doing, however, he appears to overlook the way in which the process of fragmentation of the mental apparatus is more than a phantasy. I
believe that one must understand the formation of bizarre
objects as involving two different sorts of mental operation. One facet of the process is simply a phantasy—a
gramophone is a mental representation that is imagined to
be capable of perception. However, this phantasy is a
thought generated by a part of the mind that has, in fact,
been split off from the "nonpsychotic" mind and is actually functioning as an active, separate suborganization of
the personality that experiences itself as a thing (see
Ogden, 1980, 1982b). I understand the gramophone image
to be equivalent to a self-representation of this aspect of
the personality.

Grotstein (1981, 1983) has built upon Bion's theory

of the simultaneous functioning of psychotic and nonpsychotic parts of the personality to construct a "dual track model" of the mind in which experience is no longer conceived of as unitary, but as an overlapping of two or more separate experiences generated by autonomous suborganizations of the personality. Only through integration of various experiential perspectives is the illusion of unitary experience created, much as an integrated visual field with visual depth is achieved through an integration of slightly different visual images perceived by each eye. Grotstein's proposal represents an important rediscovery of one of Freud's most fundamental contributions to psychology. Freud proposed that we view the human mind as consisting of two facets, the conscious and the unconscious mind. Although these two aspects of mind function in different modes (primary and secondary process), they operate concurrently and together contribute to the generation of experience that feels unitary to the subject. This sense of unity of experience is achieved despite the fact that the conscious and unconscious aspects of mind are operating semiautonomously.

A Revised Theory of Internal Objects

Before presenting an integration of the foregoing contributions to a theory of internal objects, I will briefly recapitulate the critical turning points in the development of this aspect of psychoanalytic theory. Melanie Klein was the first to establish a conception of an internal object world organized around internal object relationships, consisting of an unconscious split-off aspect of ego in relation to an internal object. Her theory suffered from an unsatisfactory formulation of the theoretical status of internal objects, which were conceived of as unconscious phantasies but were at the same time thought of as capable of thinking, feeling, perceiving, and responding. Fairbairn clarified the matter by stating that neither objects nor object representations are internalized; rather, that which is internalized is an object relationship consisting of a split-off part of the ego in relation to an object which is itself, at least in part, a dynamic structure. The split-off aspect of the ego retains the capacity to function as an active psychological agency, although it functions in a primitive mode due to its relative isolation from other aspects of the developing personality. Fairbairn, although designating internal objects dynamic structures, did not explain how an internal object (presumably originally a thought) achieves its dynamism. Winnicott extended the notion of splitting of the ego to include subdivisions of the experience of self but did not contribute to a clarification of the concept of internal objects.

Bion's theory of the pathological formation of bizarre objects provided an important insight into the formation of all internal objects. He envisioned a defensive splitting of the mind into parts that include active suborganizations of the mind, which then experience themselves as having become things. Thus, the formation of a bizarre object is a process by which a suborganization of the mind engages in a specific object-related phantasy involving feelings of merger with, or entrapment by, the object.

On the basis of these contributions to object relations theory, I shall now attempt to clarify the theoretical status of internal objects in a way that will facilitate clinical thinking about various transference and resistance phenomena. An internal object relationship necessarily involves an interaction between two subdivisions of the personality, each subdivision capable of being an active psychological agency. Otherwise, one's theory must posit either a direct relationship between nonequivalent levels of abstraction, e.g., the ego (a structure) in a relationship with an object representation (a thought) or a relationship between two thoughts, which would necessarily give thoughts the power to think. Freud's recognition of the fact that two active agencies are required for an internal object relationship is reflected in his theory of superego formation wherein the ego is seen as split into two active organizations in an internal relationship with one another.

Fairbairn's insight that object relationships, rather than objects, are internalized opened the way to thinking of both the self- and the object-components of the internal relationship as active agencies, "dynamic structures." The self-component was understood as a split-off aspect of the ego, thus accounting for its capacity to think, perceive, and respond. However, although Fairbairn recognized that theoretical consistency demanded that the object-component of the internal object relationship also be considered a dynamic structure, he did not offer an explanation for the source of the dynamism of the internal object. Applying Bion's theory of the formation of pathological bizarre objects to the formation of internal objects in general, one can conceptualize internal objects as split-off aspects of the ego that have been "projected into" mental representations of objects; an aspect of ego is split off and becomes profoundly identified with an object representation. Because the ego suborganization is itself capable of generating meanings, its identification with an object representation results in a shift in the way that aspect of the person thinks of itself. That which was originally an object representation becomes experientially equivalent to a self-representation of one of the split-off facets of ego.

In this light, I suggest that the internalization of an object relationship be thought of as necessarily involving a dual subdivision of the ego. *Such a dual split would result in the formation of two new suborganizations of the ego, one*

*identified with the self in the external object relationship and
the other thoroughly identified with the object.* This formulation accounts for the dynamic nature of the internal object and also defines the relationship between the concept
of ego and the concept of internal objects. In brief, internal objects are subdivisions of the ego that are heavily
identified with an object representation while maintaining
the capacities of the whole ego for thought, perception,
and feeling. Such a proposal goes no further in the direction of demonology than did Freud in describing the formation of the superego.

The logical extension of Fairbairn's theory of dynamic structure is that the ego is the only source of dynamism and that further dynamic structures are formed only
by a subdivision of the ego. The dynamism of an internal
object must in every case reflect the fact that an aspect of
the ego has been split off and is at the core of the new
structure. The fact that this structure (the internal object)
is experienced as nonself is accounted for by means of its
profound identification with the object. Internalization
requiring a splitting of the ego occurs only in early development, and, as a result, the identification with the object
is of a poorly differentiated nature. The experiential quality of the identification is one of "becoming the object" as
opposed to "feeling like" the object. Adult "internaliza-
tions" are built upon existing splits in the ego and do not
involve the creation of new ones.

Transference, Countertransference, and Projective Identification

From the perspective of the view of internal object relations presented above, transference and countertransference can now be understood as the interpersonal exter-

nalization ("actualization," Ogden, 1980, 1982b) of an internal object relationship. Transference can take one of two forms, depending on whether it is the role of the object or that of the self in the internal object relationship that is assigned to another person in the externalization process. When it is the role of the internal object that is projected, the patient experiences another person as he has unconsciously experienced that internal object (an unconscious split-off part of the ego identified with the object). In such a case, countertransference involves the therapist's unconscious identification with that aspect of the patient's ego identified with the object (Racker's "complementary identification" [1957]).

Projective identification involves *in addition* an interpersonal pressure on the therapist to engage in such an identification. The "recipient" (e.g., the therapist) is coerced into seeing himself only as the object represented in the internal object relationship. More accurately, there is an attempt to make the recipient's experience congruent with the way in which the internal object (aspect of the ego) *experiences itself* and perceives the self-component of the internal relationship. The subject unconsciously phantasizes that he ejects part of himself and enters the object in a controlling way.

Transference

This form of externalization in which another person is treated as if he were the object-component of an internal object relationship is the process that is generally referred to as transference. For example, a 20-year-old patient maintained a fearful but defiant internal relationship in which one aspect of ego was locked in battle with another split-off aspect of ego identified with a bullying father representation. This patient was preoccupied with his anxiety about a particular male teacher, whom he experienced as extremely intimidating. Nevertheless, the patient would struggle against unconscious wishes to undermine and "show up" the teacher in class. Such a transference relationship (based on the externalization of the object-component of the internal relationship) became a projective identification as the patient began to imagine being able to "push the buttons" of the teacher in an omnipotent way and would in reality provoke the teacher into a bullying stance.

The other of the two forms of transference described occurs when the patient experiences another person (e.g., the therapist) in the same way the internal object (split-off portion of ego identified with the object) experiences the aspect of the ego identified with self. The countertransference in this case consists of the therapist's identification with the self-component of the patient's internal object relationship (Racker's "concordant identification" [1957]). Projective identification would in this case involve, in addition, an unconscious phantasy of projecting the self-component into the external object together with interpersonal pressure on the object for compliance with this phantasy, i.e., pressure on the external object to experience himself only as the internal object experiences the self in the internal object relationship.

The externalization of the self-component of an internal object relationship was exemplified by a psychotic adolescent who was continually tormented by intrusive obsessional thoughts, accusatory auditory hallucinations, and feelings that his mind was being controlled. He felt that he could not find a single moment of reprieve from these internal emotional assaults. The patient was seen in intensive individual psychotherapy in a long-term psychiatric hospital. In the course of this work, the patient's current experience came to be understood as an internal version of his experience of his relationship with his mother, who had regularly, secretly observed him for hours at nursery school, had given him placebo medication for his "nerves," and had tape-recorded his dinner conversation and temper tantrums to play back to him for "study" later. He had been sent to a family friend for "therapy." Following each session, the "therapist" would report to the parents about what had transpired.

In the psychotherapy occurring during the patient's hospitalization, the patient subjected the therapist to a continual verbal and sensory barrage. In a relentless, loud, whiny, highly pressured tone of voice, he would make incessant demands of the therapist. When not gratified, the patient would call the therapist a string of mocking names that were repeated so often and so loudly that a 50-minute session felt to the therapist like being subjected to the din of a jack hammer for hours. The therapist not only felt angry, but also experienced feelings of disorganization and utter helplessness that at times gave him the panicky feeling that he was drowning. The patient described these sessions as "negative mind control games," a term which referred to the idea that efforts at controlling his mind were "jammed" and the jamming in turn had the effect of sending the mind control back to its source.

In this example, the self-component of an internal object relationship (in which the patient experienced himself as violently intruded upon by his mother) was projected into the therapist. The phantasy of negative mind control was accompanied by an interpersonal interaction that served to induce in the therapist the experience of the self in the internal object relationship. The phantasy, the interpersonal pressure, and the therapist's resonant response together constituted a projective identification.

The following is another example of the type of transference involving the externalization of the self-component of the internal object relationship. Robert, a 20-year-old schizophrenic patient seen in intensive psychotherapy, unconsciously engaged in a painful internal object relationship in which he felt "contaminated" by a mother who would insinuate herself into every facet of his body and mind. During an extended period of therapy, the patient refused to bathe, and as time went on the therapist became preoccupied with the patient's odor, which filled the office long after the patient had left. The therapist's office chair absorbed the patient's odor and became a symbol of the patient's entry into the therapist's life outside of the therapy hours. Thus, the therapist felt as if he himself had become inescapably suffused by the patient. In this case, the therapist had unwittingly been coerced into experiencing himself as the self-component of the internal relationship to the contaminating mother (an aspect of the patient's ego identified with this representation of the mother). (See Ogden, 1982a, for an in-depth discussion of this case.)

It is my experience that projective identification is a universal feature of the externalization of an internal object relationship, i.e., of transference. What is variable is the degree to which the external object is enlisted as a participant in the externalization of the internal object relationship. There is always a component of the therapist's response to the patient's transferences that represents an induced identification with an aspect of the patient's ego that is locked in a particular unconscious internal object relationship. This identification on the part of the therapist represents a form of understanding of the patient that can be acquired in no other way.

In my opinion, it is not possible to analyze the transference without making oneself available to participate to some degree in this form of identification. However, it is by no means sufficient to have become a participant in the externalization of an internal relationship. One must, in addition, be able to understand that which one is experiencing as a reflection of a need on the part of the patient to reduce the therapist to the status of a surrogate for a part of the patient's ego. The therapist must himself be aware that the patient is excluding all aspects of the therapist's personality that do not correspond to the features of the split-off ego with which the therapist is being identified. There is considerable psychological work involved in the therapist's consciously and unconsciously integrating the roles imposed upon him with his larger, more reality-based sense of himself (in particular, his role as therapist).

Resistance

From the perspective of this conception of internal objects, resistance is understood in terms of the difficulty the patient has in giving up the pathological attachments involved in unconscious internal object relationships. Fairbairn (1944, 1958) was the first to understand resistance in this way and placed particular emphasis on the tie to the bad internal object. This tie is based on one's need to change the bad object into the kind of person one wishes the object were.

Fairbairn (1944) described two forms of attachment to the frustrating internal object. One form is the attachment of the craving self to the tantalizing object. The nature of this tie to the object is that of the addict for the addicting agent and is extremely difficult to relinquish. (See Ogden, 1974, for a description of a psychotherapy in which the central resistance was derived from this type of internal object tie.)

The second category of bond to a bad internal object is the tie of the wronged and spoiling self to the unloving, rejecting object. This often takes the form of a crusade to expose the unfairness of, coldness of, or other forms of wrongdoing on the part of the internal object.

Fairbairn (1940) presented graphic clinical data demonstrating the phenomenon of loyalty to the bad internal object that is fueled by the unconscious conviction that a bad object is far preferable to no object at all. Fairbairn's thinking stems from the idea that a human being's sanity and survival depend on object-relatedness, and a person experiences the terror of impending annihilation when he feels that all external and internal object ties are being severed. Therefore, he clings desperately to any object tie (external or internal), even ones that are experienced as bad, when that is all that is available.

Fairbairn, because of his incomplete formulation of the nature of internal objects, focused exclusively on resistances derived from the experience of the self-component of the internal object relationship. As discussed earlier, Fairbairn only hesitantly accepted the idea that internal objects are dynamic structures and was not able to delineate the relationship between the concept of internal objects and the concept of ego. As a result, he restricted himself to studying ways in which the loyalty of the self to the internal object functions as a resistance to therapeutic work.

Other forms of resistance become recognizable from the perspective of a theory that regards internal object relations as involving two active agencies, each capable of generating experience. Not only does one encounter resistance stemming from the loyalty of the self to the bad object, one regularly encounters resistance based on the object's need for the self. This is not to introduce a conception of an inner world occupied by internal objects flying about one's mind on their own steam. From the perspective of the present chapter, these internal objects are understood as aspects of the ego identified with objects, and as such can enter into a tormenting, tantalizing, humiliating, dependent or any other form of relatedness to other aspects of the ego. Freud himself used such words to describe the relationship of the superego to the ego. Resistance to giving up internal object ties can thus be seen to stem both from those aspects of ego experienced as self and from those aspects of ego identified with objects. The latter set of resistances have not been nearly as well recognized nor elucidated.

Heretofore, focus has been placed almost exclusively on the experience of the self in relation to objects in internal object relations. This has been so largely because the object component has been conceptualized primarily as a mental representation (an idea), and therefore, it would not make sense to talk about the way in which a thought experiences a change in an internal object relationship. However, from the perspective of the object as suborganization of the ego, one is in a position to think about the following aspects of resistance stemming from the unwillingness of the object to relinquish its tie to other aspects of the ego involved in internal object relationships:

1. The ego suborganization identified with the object is under constant pressure from the self-component of the relationship to be transformed into a good object. Such a

transformation is strenuously resisted by the object-component, because this type of massive shift in identity would be experienced as the annihilation of an aspect of the ego. The internal object relationship is vigorously defended from two directions: The self-component is unwilling to risk annihilation resulting from absence of object relatedness and instead strives to change the bad object into a good one; at the same time, the object-component fends off annihilation that would result from being transformed into a new entity (the good object). It is this latter motivation that accounts for the often encountered moment in therapy when the patient pleadingly looks at the therapist and says, "I know that what I am doing is self-defeating, but to stop thinking and acting in that way would require that I become somebody else and I can't do that. I wouldn't recognize myself when I look in the mirror."

In work with borderline and schizophrenic patients, this form of resistance often underlies the patient's intensely conflicted feelings about accepting the therapist's interpretations. Frequently, the transference relationship in such circumstances involves an externalization of an internal object relationship of the following type: the analyst is experienced as the self-component of the internal relationship in which the self is intent on changing the object-component at the cost of annihilating that aspect of the patient. For example, a schizophrenic patient over many years of therapy would periodically become psychotic and regress profoundly to the point of entering an almost totally mute, immobile state that would last for many months. These regressions occurred just as the patient began to "get better." "Improvement" was experienced by the patient as literally becoming the therapist and in so doing losing himself entirely. Stubborn passivity evidenced by the patient at such points was an unconscious assertion that the therapist could not induce, seduce, manipulate, or coerce the patient into changing into the person that the therapist "wanted" or "needed" the patient to be. "Getting better" meant being transformed into somebody else and no longer existing as the person he felt himself to be.

Interpretations are regularly experienced by schizophrenic and borderline patients as placing the patient in a terrible dilemma: to listen (in phantasy to "take in") is to risk becoming changed into the therapist; not to listen (in phantasy to "refuse to take in") is experienced as risking losing all connection with the therapist and as a result floating off into absolute "outer-space-like" isolation. Either way, the patient's existence is threatened. The danger of losing one's self as a result of being transformed into a "good" object is the danger experienced by the object-component of the internal relationship; the risk of absolute isolation resulting from loss of the connection with the internal object is the danger experienced by the self-component of the internal object relationship. It is as important for the object-component of ego in the internal relationship to resist being changed by the self-component as it is for the self-component to attempt to change the bad object into a good one.

2. The suborganization of ego identified with the object experiences as much need for object relatedness as the self-component of the internal object relationship. The object-component frequently maintains internal object ties by means of attempting to exert control over its object (i.e., control over the self-component of the internal relationship). The object-component may taunt, shame, threaten, dominate, or induce guilt in its object (the self-

component of the internal relationship) in order to maintain connectedness with the self-component. These efforts
at control over the self-component become greatly intensi-
fied when there is danger of the bond being threatened,
e.g., by a more mature form of relatedness to the therapist
that would make this internal, more primitive form of
relatedness less necessary.[5]

An obsessional patient in intensive psychotherapy
would regularly disrupt her rare periods of genuine self-
analytic free association with "outbreaks" of obsessional
self-torment. For instance, while insightfully discussing
an interchange with a boyfriend, she interrupted her train
of thought to ruminate self-critically about her weight, a
subject with which she was chronically preoccupied. As
the ruminations continued she became anxious that the
therapist would terminate therapy because of her endless
and fruitless obsessional thinking. The patient was at this
point in therapy aware of the connection between her self-
torment and the way in which she had continually felt
belittled and tormented by her mother. The patient's
mother, in addition to tirelessly pointing out her disdain
for the patient, regularly threatened to send her away to
live with relatives. (It must be emphasized that it is the
patient's experience of her mother, not an objective depic-

---

[5]The unconscious self and object suborganizations of the ego are
affected to some extent by current experience. Self suborganizations
of the ego are influenced by experience, particularly as the current
experience involves issues of goals, ambitions, and autonomy. Object
suborganizations are influenced by current relations with external
objects particularly with regard to issues of idealization, denigration,
jealousy, envy, etc. One measure of psychological health is the degree
to which internal object relations can be modified in the light of
current experience.

tion of the mother, that is preserved in the internal object relationship.)

The internal object relationship upon which the transference was modeled consisted of a mutually dependent mother-child relationship in which the child was willing and eager to be masochistic if that would help solidify the tie to a sadistic mother who was felt to be always on the verge of abandoning her. The internal object (suborganization of the ego) experienced the ability of other aspects of the patient to engage in free association in the therapeutic setting as dangerous evidence of an enhanced capacity of those other aspects of the ego to engage in a more mature form of relatedness to the therapist. The fear of this more mature form of object tie resulted from the object's conviction that such relatedness would make the self-component of the internal object relationship less dependent on the object-component. In the clinical sequence described, the object (suborganization of ego) then redoubled its efforts to subject the masochistic self to sadistic torment in the form of guilt-inducing taunts about being overweight. The nature of the ultimate threat made by the object-component is that of abandoning the self-component of the internal relationship. In the clinical sequence, the threat of abandonment is projected onto the therapist and is experienced as a threat made by the therapist to abandon the patient if she does not behave as he demands.

In this clinical material, the resistance (the disruption of the free association) arose from the fear of giving up a particular internal object relationship. This fear is predominantly that of the object (ego suborganization) which, upon sensing decreasing dependence on the part of the self-component, reintensified its efforts to control by raising the spectre of abandonment. In the context of an internal object relationship, any independent activity on the part of one party of the relationship is experienced as an impending dissolution of the relationship which is based on mutual dependence. From the perspective of the patient's unconscious psychic reality, it is as essential for the object-component of ego in an internal relationship to maintain its tie to the self-component as it is for the self-component to tirelessly pursue and attempt to hold onto the internal object.

3. Feelings of envy experienced by the object-component and directed at the self-component of an internal object relationship constitute another type of internal object-relatedness that can serve as the basis for resistance. Not infrequently we hear patients expressing envy toward others at times when it does not make immediate sense in terms of the patient's current situation. For example, a borderline patient who had been in intensive psychotherapy for four years was able for the first time in a decade to return to school and to relate to her second husband in a way in which she was taking some pride. She had abandoned her latency-aged children when she left her first husband fifteen years previously. In her current therapy meetings, in addition to discussing the enhanced feelings of self-worth, she reported having written an extremely angry letter to her children. As she talked about this, she said that she had been a much better mother to them than her own mother (who had committed suicide when she was 10 years old) had been to her. It became abundantly clear to the patient that she was feeling intensely envious of her children. From the point of view of the self in an internal object relationship with a deeply depressed, rejecting mother, envy is not a feeling one

would expect at a time when the patient is experiencing enhanced self-esteem. However, from the point of view of the object (the patient's ego suborganization identified with her mother), not only is control over the self-component threatened by enhanced feelings of self-esteem, the object also feels envious of the self for this newly acquired set of feelings. The object-component, in order to maintain a tie (based on control) over the self-component, wished to sap the feelings of well-being from its object (the self) and make those feelings its own. It is vitally important for the object to maintain connectedness with the self. Signs of diminished dependence on the part of the self will be enviously attacked as the object (suborganization of ego) begins to fear being left behind.

Searles (1979) vividly described similar clinical data in which the patient unconsciously functions as multiple people, one of whom may become jealous of the other. He gives detailed accounts of the way in which such internal splitting may be externalized as a countertransference experience in which one aspect of the therapist feels jealous of another aspect of himself that is felt to be more desirable to the patient. Searles (1979) concurs with Fairbairn that, although such internal divisions are more apparent in borderline and schizoid individuals, "it would take a bold man to claim that his ego was so perfectly integrated as to be incapable of revealing any evidence of splitting at the deepest levels, or that such evidence of splitting of the ego could in no circumstances declare itself at more superficial levels, even under conditions of extreme suffering or hardship or deprivation" (Fairbairn, 1940, p. 8).

Searles focuses entirely on jealousy of the self for another aspect of self. The theoretical framework of the present chapter allows us to supplement Searles's ideas with a way of thinking about types of resistance based on jealousy or envy of an internal object for the self.

Summary

The concept of internal object relations is first approached in this chapter through a study of its historical development. Freud's theory of superego formation involves the notion of a splitting of the ego (in the context of the child's identification with an external object) followed by the establishment of a relationship between the two resultant aspects of ego. Melanie Klein contributed the notion of an internal object world organized around the relationships of split-off aspects of ego to internal objects. However, Klein's writing is fraught with contradictions about whether internal objects are to be viewed as phantasies, active agencies, or both. Fairbairn insisted that object relationships, not objects, are internalized and that internal objects are at least in part dynamic structures. He fully established for the first time the notion that all internal object relationships involve two active agencies. However, the source of the dynamism of objects was left unexplained. Bion's theory of bizarre objects provides a model for thinking about the way in which an aspect of the mind may become split off and engage in a profound identification with an inanimate object, leading to the feeling that it has become "a thing."

On the basis of these developments, I have proposed that a dual split in the ego is required for the establishment of an internal object relationship. One split-off aspect of ego is identified with the self in the original object relationship; another is thoroughly identified with the object. The concepts of transference, countertransference, and projective identification are then viewed from this perspective.

Resistance is understood as the difficulty a patient has in relinquishing pathological attachments involved in unconscious internal object relationships. The view of internal objects proposed in this chapter brings into focus types of resistance that had formerly been only partially understood. These types of resistance are based on the need of the internal object (suborganization of ego) not to be changed by the self (suborganization of ego), the dependence of the internal object on the self, and the envy and jealousy of the internal object for the self-component of the internal object relationship.

7

The Mother, the Infant, and the Matrix in the Work of Donald Winnicott

A book which does not contain its counterbook is considered incomplete.

—Jorge Luis Borges, *"Tlön, Uqbar, Orbis, Tertius"*

Donald Winnicott developed his contribution to the psychoanalytic dialogue in the intellectual and social climate of the British Psychoanalytical Society during the 1920s through the early 1970s. During much of this period, the British Society was sharply and often bitterly divided between the ideas and personalities of Anna Freud and Melanie Klein. Winnicott was analyzed first by James Strachey and then by Joan Rivière, one of the early Kleinian "inner circle"; he was supervised by Melanie Klein in his psychoanalytic work with children. Although Winni-

167

cott's thinking developed in a direction different from that of Klein, he never denounced Kleinian thinking, as did many analysts who had at one point been open to her ideas (e.g., Glover [1945] and Schmideberg [1935]).

Winnicott was a dialectician. His thinking thrived in the medium of the intense debate between the classical Freudian and the Kleinian groups. He understood that once we feel that we have finally resolved a basic psychoanalytic issue (either in our theory or in our understanding of patients), our thinking has reached an impasse. Winnicott (1968) states, I think without false humility, that he offered his patients interpretations to let them know the limits of his understanding. Many of Winnicott's most valuable clinical and theoretical contributions are in the form of paradoxes that he asks us to accept without resolving, for the truth of the paradox lies in neither of its poles, but in the space between them.

Object relations theory is not composed of a discrete collection of principles: rather, it represents a diverse collection of contributions that, in my opinion, have been developed in the context of one of the most intense and fruitful of psychoanalytic dialogues. In this chapter I will focus on the nature of the infant's dependence on the mother as this concept emerges from the work of Donald Winnicott. I believe that Winnicott's understanding of the mother's role in early development becomes fully accessible only when it is approached from the vantage point of the dialogue with Klein within which his ideas were developed. The Winnicottian ideas that will be discussed are not simply refutations of Klein, nor revisions of Klein, nor extensions of Klein. These contributions are ideas generated in response to a rich epistemologic dilemma created in large part by the Kleinian contribution. The next three sections of this chapter explore three different forms of Winnicott's conception of the infant's evolving dependence on the mother. There will be an attempt, through the clarification, interpretation, and extension of Winnicott's ideas, to make more fully accessible for analytic consideration important meanings implicit in this facet of Winnicott's work.

I. The Period of the Subjective Object

Although Klein did not ignore the role of the mother, Winnicott did not believe that Klein understood the nature of the mother–infant relationship.

> She [Klein] paid lip-service to environmental provision, but would never fully acknowledge that along with the dependence of early infancy is truly a period in which it is not possible to describe an infant without describing the mother whom the infant has not yet become able to separate from a self. Klein claimed to have paid full attention to the environmental factor, but it is my opinion that she was temperamentally incapable of this. (Winnicott, 1962a, p. 177)

The specific qualities of the interpersonal relationship between mother and infant play a role secondary to that of phantasy in Kleinian thinking even though, for Klein, phantasy is always object related in content. The mother as she actually exists is seen by Klein as eclipsed by the phantasied mother who is constructed by the infant on the basis of the infant's projections: "The child's earliest reality is wholly-phantastic" (Klein, 1930, p. 238). The idea that the infant is isolated from what an observer would consider reality is not what Winnicott objects to in

Kleinian theory. Rather, Winnicott's objection is to what he views as Klein's failure to examine the nature of the influence on psychological development of the infant's dependence on the mother. Klein's focus was almost exclusively on psychological contents: their origins in biology (instinctual deep structure), their intrapsychic elaboration (e.g., by means of splitting, projection, introjection, omnipotent thought, idealization, and denial), and their interpersonal transformations (by means of projective and introjective identification). Winnicott was not unaware of the potential for an interpersonal dimension to Klein's concept of projective identification. However, projective identification was for Klein primarily a process by which psychological contents were modified; it was not intended to address the basic unity of maternal and infantile psychology.

Klein (1946, 1948, 1957) viewed the infant as a distinct psychological entity from birth. Psychological development was understood by her as a series of biologically determined defensive transformations engaged in by the infant to *take care of himself* in the face of internal and external danger. In contrast, Winnicott's theory of development is not a depiction of defensive adjustments made by an infant in the face of danger. Rather, it is an exploration of the mother's provision of protective postponement and dosed stimulation. When the infant is in the womb, the mother's role is to provide an environment that will buy the infant the time that he needs to mature before having to face the inevitable task of physical separation at birth. In precisely the same way, the mother's role in the first months of life (prior to the infant's entry into the period of the transitional phenomena at "about four to six to eight to twelve months" [Winnicott, 1951, p. 4]), is to provide an environment in which the postponement of

psychological separateness can occur while the infant develops as a result of the interplay of biological maturation
and actual experience. (As will be discussed, a crucial part
of this interplay involves dosed stimulation including frustration.) The fact that the infant can develop only in the
protective, postponing[1] envelope of the maternal environment constitutes one level of the meaning of Winnicott's
(1960a) notion that "there is no such thing as an infant"
(p. 39 fn.).

Mother-Infant Unit

A new psychological entity is created by mother and infant
that is not the outcome of a process of simple summation
of parts. The situation is more akin to the interaction of
two elements reacting with one another to generate a new
entity, a compound. It is the "compound," the mother-
infant, that is the unit of psychological development for
Winnicott: "The behaviour of the environment is part of

---

[1]I am aware that I am reversing the usual way of viewing a developmental sequence. Ordinarily, an earlier developmental phase is
thought of as preparatory for the succeeding one. I am suggesting that
an earlier developmental phase also forestalls the next one. Clearly,
no intentionality is being attributed to the biological function of
postponement.

Psychology is not merely an epiphenomenon of biology: biology
and psychology are inseparable facets of a single developmental/
maturational process. Early stages of psychological maturation and
development serve to help the organism manage in a state of biological
immaturity and in this sense secure the organism time to mature.
Freud's (1895, 1896b, 1918) concept of "deferred action" (*nachtra-
glich*) speaks to the same point: for example, "The retardation of
puberty makes possible posthumous primary processes" (1895,
p. 359).

the individual's own personal development" (Winnicott, 1971e, p. 53).

Since the mother-infant is a psychological entity contributed to by (what an outside observer would designate as) the mother and the infant, the unit of psychological development is always both a primitive psychological organization and a relatively mature one. In this sense, all levels of psychological development are represented in the psyche of the mother-infant. (This accounts for the presence of the implicit synchronic developmental axis in Winnicott's thinking that will be described.) The study of psychological development is not simply the study of the growth of the infantile psyche from primitivity to maturity; it is also the study of the development of the mother-infant into a mother and infant.

An aspect of the mother is mixed up with the infant in a state that Winnicott refers to as "primary maternal preoccupation" (1956). This experience of losing oneself in another ("feeling herself into her infant's place" [p. 304]) is the mother's experience of becoming a part of the mother-infant. If there is no aspect of the mother that is at one with the infant, the infant is experienced as a foreign object. One such mother referred to her baby as "the thing that lives in my house." (Of course, there is an element of this feeling of alienation in the spectrum of emotions experienced by most mothers.) If there is no aspect of the mother outside of the experience of primary maternal preoccupation, the mother has in fact become psychotic. Under such circumstances, separation from the baby is concretely experienced as a form of amputation.

For Winnicott (1951, 1962b), psychological development does not begin with the unfolding of a biologically predetermined set of psychological functions by which the infant takes care of himself in the face of anxiety; rather, early development centers around the mother's initial provision of the illusion of the "subjective object," i.e., the creation of the illusion that internal and external reality are one and the same. The mother is able, in her state of primary maternal preoccupation, to provide the infant with what he needs, in the way that he needs it, when he needs it, as if he had "created' the object.

The illusion of "invisible oneness." Winnicott's (1951) use of the idea of the illusion of "creating the breast" is somewhat confusing if the notion of creating the breast is thought to involve an awareness of otherness. In the beginning, the illusion created by the mother is not an illusion of the infant's omnipotent power to create what is needed; rather, the illusion is that need does not exist. I believe that the idea of "invisible oneness" (see Chapter 8) of mother and infant is perhaps more expressive of the form of experience that Winnicott is proposing than is the idea of the infant's creating the breast.

The creation of the breast is an observable phenomenon only from a point of view outside of the mother–infant unit. Within the mother–infant unit, the creation of the breast is not noticed, because the infant in this state does not yet have a point of view from which to notice anything. In a homogeneous field, there are no vantage points, no foreground or background. Without difference, there can be no perspective. The mother's caretaking is good enough when it is so unobtrusive as to be unnoticed. Even the stimulation needed by the infant and provided by the mother is unnoticed at first. The infant's ability to be sensorally alive and to make complex discriminations (see Stern, 1977) is not the same as awareness of self or of other. The delaying of the infant's awareness of separateness is achieved in large part by means of the mother's meeting of the infant's need before need becomes desire.

The infant without desire is neither a subject nor an object: there is not yet an infant.

Because Winnicott's thinking involves a subtle mixture of explicit diachronic[2] conceptions of development and implicit synchronic notions, the idea that the mother must at the outset protect the infant from awareness of desire is an incomplete representation of Winnicott's thinking. It is true that Winnicott (1945, 1971a) repeatedly states that in the beginning the mother must meet the infant's needs and in so doing protect the baby from premature awareness of separateness. In this conception of things, separateness follows oneness in a sequential, chronological way. At other times, however, Winnicott (1954–1955, 1963) states that mothering, even at the beginning, must not be too good. The infant is robbed of the experience of desire if his every need is anticipated and met before it is experienced, for example, as appetite. Even under normal circumstances, the meeting of the infant's needs forecloses important possibilities at the same time that it satisfies and protects the infant.

[2]A diachronic developmental axis involves a linear, sequential conception of development in which one phase of development builds upon the previous one through processes that include structural differentiation, integration, and epigenetic unfolding of maturational potentials. Freud's (1905) sequence of psychosexual phases, Anna Freud's (1965) conception of developmental lines, Piaget's (1946) notion of stepwise development of cognitive structures through assimilation and accommodation, and Erikson's (1950) conception of an epigenetic unfolding of psychosocial stages, are all examples of diachronic conceptions of development. A synchronic developmental axis involves a conception of coexisting hierarchically interrelated levels of development. Freud's (1896b, 1918) conception of "stratification," Klein's (1932b) notion of the spreading of libidinal excitation between levels of development, and Lacan's (1957) conception of the imaginary and symbolic orderings of experience, represent synchronic developmental conceptions.

The baby is fobbed off by the feed itself; instinct tension disappears, and the baby is both satisfied and cheated. It is too easily assumed that a feed is followed by satisfaction and sleep. Often distress follows this fobbing off, especially if physical satisfaction too quickly robs the infant of zest. The infant is then left with: aggression undischarged—because not enough muscle erotism or primitive impulse (motility), was used in the feeding process; or a sense of "flop"— since the source of zest for life has gone suddenly, and the infant does not know it will return. (Winnicott, 1954-1955, p. 268)

So it is not sufficient to say that the mother must in the beginning meet the infant's needs in order to protect the infant from premature knowledge of separateness (a diachronic statement). Neither is it sufficient to say that the mother from the beginning must meet the infant's need for "zest" in allowing the infant the opportunity to develop desire through the experience of partially unfulfilled needs. Only a paradoxical statement in which both the synchronic and diachronic axes are represented can approach completeness: the mother must shield the infant from awareness of desire and separateness, *and* the mother must safeguard the infant's opportunity to experience desire and the accompanying knowledge of separateness.

Instinct, Defense and Individuality

Central to Winnicottian (1971a) developmental theory is the idea that there is a potential individuality at birth and that the mother (both as environment and as object) facilitates the development of that unfolding individuality. In large part, the task of the mother is not to interfere with the infant's spontaneous development that begins as a state of "formless" (1971d, p. 64) "going on being". The development of the psychological system is not predominantly propelled by the need to find channels for the discharge of instinctual tension (as in Freud's energy model) nor by the need to defend against danger posed by the death instinct (as in Kleinian theory).

This is not to say that Winnicott rejected either instinct theory or the notion of the central role of anxiety in the normal structuring of the psyche in general, and of the ego in particular. For Winnicott, it is all a matter of the timing of the handing over of caretaking (including defensive operations) from the mother (more accurately, the mother–infant) to the infant. If there is a premature rupture of the holding environment, the infant too early becomes a reactive creature, and develops hypertrophied, rigid defensive structures. Under such circumstances, the infant must attempt to deal with psychological tasks that he is not yet maturationally equipped to manage. On the other hand, if the holding environment is "too good" for too long, the infant is prevented from experiencing dosed frustration, tolerable anxiety, desire, and conflict, and as a result will not develop ways of caring for himself (including defending himself psychologically). All of these qualities of experience—frustration, anxiety, desire, conflicted desire—introduce difference and lead to internal differentiation. The creation of the unconscious mind (and therefore, the conscious mind) becomes possible and necessary only in the face of conflicted desire that leads to the need to disown and yet preserve aspects of experience, i.e., the need to maintain two different modes of experiencing the same psychological event simultaneously. In other words, the very existence of the differentiation of the conscious and unconscious mind stems from a conflict between a desire to feel/think/be in specific ways, and the desire not to feel/think/be in those ways.

For Winnicott, the ability of the infant to make use of the integrating and structuring effects of instinctual experience (including instinctual conflict) depends upon the mother's success in postponing (and yet preserving) the infant's awareness of desire, and therefore of conflicted desire, until, and not beyond, the point where the infant experiences his feelings as his own. Prior to that point, "the instincts can be as external as a clap of thunder or a hit" (Winnicott, 1960a, p. 141), and will disrupt the infant's developing sense of internally generated desire. Once a sense of self has begun to consolidate (in the way that will be described below), instinctual experience serves to focus and organize the infant's sense of himself as author of his experience (Winnicott, 1967a). One's being takes specific form in the process of feeling and acting upon one's desires.

The Defensive Preservation of the Self

When there is a prolonged and serious failure to provide a good enough holding environment,[3] the infant is thrown into a state of chaos and disruption of his sense of "going on being" (Winnicott, 1963, p. 183). The outcome is childhood psychosis or the nucleus of adult psychotic or borderline states. When the failure of the holding environment is less severe, the infant may be able to develop a defensive personality organization that takes over the caretaking function of the mother. This organization is devel-

[3]It is important to emphasize that inadequacy of mothering is only one of the possible causes of failure of the holding environment. Other important causes include prematurity of birth, physical illness of the infant, unusual sensitivity on the part of the infant, and "lack of fit" between the temperaments of a particular mother and a particular infant.

oped in a state of perceived danger. Instead of the mutually enriching interplay that results from the differentiation of the conscious and unconscious minds and the establishment of a "semipermeable" repression barrier, there develops an alienation of one aspect of self from another (Winnicott, 1960b, 1963). The defensive, caretaking self (the False Self) is established almost exclusively for the purpose of securing the protective isolation of the infant's potential for psychological individuality (the True Self). This isolation of the True Self inevitably leads to feelings of emptiness, futility, and deadness. The walling-off of a protected self stands in contrast to the dual role of censorship and selective, disguised expression performed by the unconscious ego in normal development. The difference between normally developing defenses and a psychological split leading to the development of a False Self defensive organization lies in the fact that normally developing defenses enable the individual not only to organize and disavow experience, but also to unconsciously preserve disavowed desires that are nonetheless one's own. In contrast, the formation of a False Self personality organization forecloses the development of significant aspects of what might have become oneself.

II. The Period of Transitional Phenomena

Although the paradox of oneness and separateness of mother and infant has its origin in the earliest period of development, there is a shift in the quality of this dialectical relationship in the period of development in which transitional phenomena occur. It is to this period that I would now like to turn. Here again, Winnicott's thinking is in part a response to the Kleinian contribution.

The Infant's Psychological Matrix

In both the Kleinian and Winnicottian conceptions of development there is a notion that the infant in the beginning requires insulation from external reality. For Winnicott, the insulation is generated by the maternal provision of the illusion of the subjective object. The infant as conceived of by Klein (1930) is insulated by a "wholly phantastic" reality. The Kleinian infant sees the world through the lens of phylogenetically determined preconceptions and in this sense "creates" his internal and external object world, which are at first indistinguishable from each other. This is the Kleinian version of the infant's "protective shield" (Freud, 1920, p. 30).

The following question then arises in Winnicottian, Freudian, and Kleinian developmental theory: given that the infant is initially insulated from external reality, how is the infant able to utilize actual experience in the process of emerging from his initial state of isolation?[4] Here again, Winnicott's contribution to the psychoanalytic understanding of the developmental process involves a shift in perspective (a restatement of the epistemologic problem) from an attempt to understand the development of the infant to an attempt to understand the development of the mother–infant. Neither Klein nor Freud was oblivious to

[4]Freud (1900, 1911) understood early psychological development as involving a move from an initial solipsistic world of hallucinatory wish fulfillment. This is viewed as the outcome of the interplay of the biological maturation of the organism and actual experience with objects. The infant at first utilizes hallucinatory wish fulfillment to insulate himself from frustrating external reality. However, as the infant matures biologically, he shifts from efforts to create gratifying reality hallucinatorily to an effort to utilize actual experience of frustration to find other, more effective, adaptive, and indirect ways of gratifying instinctual needs.

the role of the mother (as object), but it was not until
Winnicott that psychoanalysis developed a conception of
the mother as the infant's psychological matrix.[5] *From a*
Winnicottian perspective, the infant's psychological contents
can be understood only in relation to the psychological matrix
within which those contents exist. That matrix is at first
provided by the mother. This is a second level of meaning
(to be added to the inseparability of the infant from the
protective, postponing function of the maternal holding
environment) of Winnicott's notion that there is no such
thing as an infant. Because the internal holding environment of the infant, his own psychological matrix, takes
time to develop, the infant's mental contents initially exist
within the matrix of the maternal mental and physical
activity. In other words, in the beginning, the environmental mother provides the mental space in which the
infant begins to generate experience. It is in this sense
that I feel that a new psychological entity is created by the
mother and (what is becoming) the infant.[6]

Even though aspects of the infant's psychological
contents may be experienced as things in themselves (see
Chapter 3) and thus may in themselves be quite imper-
vious to new experience, the infant's psychological matrix

---

[5]The word "matrix" is derived from the Latin word for womb. Although Winnicott (1958a) only once used the word "matrix" in his
written work (when he referred to ego-relatedness as the "matrix of
transference"), it seems to me that *matrix* is a particularly apt word to
describe the silently active containing space in which psychological
and bodily experience occur.

[6]Lacan's (1956a) concept of "the Other" similarly refers to a third
psychological entity (an intersubjective entity) generated in the analytic setting that is distinct from the patient and from the analyst:
"The Other is therefore the locus in which is constituted the I who
speaks with him who hears. . . ." (p. 141).

(the maternal holding environment) is steadily changing and is highly sensitive to modification by new experience. The holding environment (psychological matrix) shifts not only in relation to the infant's changing emotional needs (e.g., a need to be held, to be calmed, to be entertained, to show off), but also in relation to the infant's shifting maturational and developmental needs (e.g., maturing motor and cognitive capacities).

The period of the transitional phenomenon could be understood as the phase of internalization by the infant (perhaps more accurately described as the appropriation to the infant) of the psychological matrix. The maternally provided psychological matrix is in a state of continual erosion from the beginning, but only after several months does the infant begin to consolidate his capacity to generate and maintain his own psychological matrix. In this period of the transitional phenomenon, the role of the mother is one of gradual disillusionment, i.e., a gradual weaning of the infant from maternal provision of the holding environment that had served as the infant's psychological matrix. In the course of this weaning process, the infant develops the capacity to be alone (Winnicott, 1958a).

The Presence of the Absent Mother

An important distinction must be made at this point in order to understand Winnicott's thinking about the development of the capacity to be alone: What is internalized in this process is not the mother as object, but the mother as environment. The premature "objectification" (discovery of the mother as object), and internalization of the object-mother lead to the establishment of an omnipotent internal-object-mother. This internalization of mother as omnipotent object is quite different from the establishment of the capacity to be alone. (The former process is often a defensive substitute for the latter.)

In the development of the capacity to be alone, the infant develops the ability to generate the space in which he lives. (This space, referred to by Winnicott as "potential space," will be discussed in detail in Chapters 8 and 9.) Until the point in development being focused upon, the mother and infant have together created this space, which is not coextensive with the universe but, rather, is a personal space. It is not exactly limited by our skin, and it is not exactly the same as our mind. In addition to these (inexact) dimensions of body and mind, this experience of a containing space includes the experience of the space in which we work creatively, the space in which we relax "formlessly," the space in which we dream,[7] and the space in which we play.

A paradoxical statement must be made about the process of the development of the individual's capacity to generate this space: the child must have the opportunity to play alone in the presence of the absent mother, and in the absence of the present mother. This paradox can be understood in the following way: the mother is absent as object, but is there as the unnoticed, but present containing space in which the child is playing. The mother must not make her presence as object too important, for this would lead the child to become addicted to her as omnipotent object. The development of the capacity to be alone is a process in which the mother's role as invisible coauthor

---

[7]Lewin (1950) refers to this "backdrop" (p. 83) upon which dreaming occurs as the "dream screen"; Khan (1972) uses the term *dream space* for this area of experiencing; Grotstein (1981) refers to this and other backgrounds of experience as the "background object of primary identification."

of potential space is taken over by (what is becoming) the child. In this sense, the healthy individual, when alone, is always in the presence of the self-generated, environmental mother.

Impending Annihilation and the Disruption of the Matrix

Although the maternal contribution to the creation of potential space is unnoticed by the infant, the disruption of this invisible provision is a highly visible event that is experienced by the infant as impending annihilation. At such times, a discrete, separate infant is precipitiously (defensively) brought into existence in order to attempt to manage the catastrophe.

Using Balint's (1968) imagery, the infant's relationship to the environmental mother is very much like the adult's relationship to air: we ordinarily take the air we breathe for granted, taking from it what we need and expelling into it what we do not need. However, if we are deprived of it for even a few moments, we become acutely and terrifyingly aware of the way in which we are utterly dependent upon it for our lives. Psychologically this corresponds to the failure of the relationship with the environmental mother leading to the calamitous intrusion of awareness of dependency on an absent mother-as-object.

The incompleteness of the process of appropriation to the infant of the psychological matrix was evidenced by a successful engineer who, having married a woman 20 years his senior, could only feel alive when he was working on his car in the garage while his wife was in the house. If she were not at home, he could not work in this engrossed state and would impatiently await her return. On the other hand, he would become enraged if she were to come into the garage while he was working. Her actual physical presence

was experienced as a violent, unwelcome intrusion
and made it impossible for him to work.

Many chronic sleep disturbances reflect an inadequate development of the internal psychological matrix.
Falling asleep involves an act of faith in our capacity to
hold our existence over time while giving up almost all
forms of conscious control. In sleep, we give ourselves
over to our internal holding environment.[8]

Addiction to the Mother as Object

Fain (1971, quoted by McDougall, 1974) has described
forms of infantile insomnia that seem to be related to
difficulties in the infant's use of the mother as environment. Some of the infants studied by Fain seem to have
become addicted to the actual physical presence of the
mother and could not sleep unless they were being held.
These infants were unable to provide themselves an internal environment for sleep. Fain has observed that the

---

[8]Nursery rhymes (often symbolically about sleeping and told at bed-
time) are replete with references to the child's fear of falling.

> Rock-a-bye baby
> On the tree-top—
> When the wind blows,
> The cradle will rock.
> When the bough breaks,
> The cradle will fall,
> And down will come baby,
> Cradle and all.

The danger here is not simply that of bodily injury, or even that of
separation anxiety; it is the danger of the disruption of the container
of sleep, the infant's partially internal and partially external psychological matrix.

mothers of many of these infants interfered with the attempts of their infants to provide themselves substitutes for her physical presence (for example, in autoerotic activities such as thumb-sucking), thus rendering the infant fully dependent upon the actual mother as object.

In my experience as a consultant to clinicians working with severely disturbed patients, I have found that therapists doing what they feel to be "supportive therapy" with borderline and schizophrenic patients are frequently engaged in the process of addicting the patient to the therapist as object. As the following example illustrates, this potential danger exists even in well-conducted analytic work with disturbed patients.

A severely disturbed borderline patient had been seen in psychotherapy three times per week for six years and had made significant progress in the course of this work. Because of a countertransference problem arising from an interplay of feelings induced by the patient's projective identifications and feelings arising from the therapist's own childhood, the therapist was finding it difficult to tolerate the patient's growing independence. When the patient, S., became anxious about his plan to enroll in a vocational program, he became pleadingly demanding that the therapist phone the agency to get information about enrollment requirements and procedures. Although S.'s associations and dream material made it clear in retrospect that he was unconsciously asking for permission to do this for himself, the therapist acquiesced to his manifest demand. Having made the phone call, the therapist in the next meeting handed the patient a sheet of paper on which he had recorded the information that he had received from the organization. S.

immediately exploded with rage, yelling obscenities at the therapist. He then stormed out of the office, terrified that he would hurt the therapist. The patient did not return to therapy for three weeks.

In the course of supervision, it was possible for the therapist to understand what had happened in the therapy and to predict that the patient would return to the therapy in a pathetic, anxious state that would be designed to reassure the therapist that the patient was utterly dependent upon him. When S. did in fact return in this way, the therapist told him that he thought S. must feel that the therapist wanted to turn him into a baby. In the course of the meeting, the therapist also said that it seemed that the patient had decided that falling apart (and thus demonstrating his need for the therapist) was a price worth paying if the alternatives were killing the therapist, leaving him, or having the therapist leave S.

The patient seemed relieved that the therapist understood something of what he had been feeling. Before the next meeting, the patient and a friend went to the rehabilitation center, where the patient picked up a copy of the enrollment procedures. On the way home he became extremely anxious and began to fear that the meeting with the therapist had been a figment of his imagination. He called the therapist in a panic, asking for an extra meeting immediately. The therapist said that he thought that S. could wait until their next scheduled meeting the next day. With that the patient's anxiety subsided.

In the case just described, the therapist had abandoned his role as provider of a therapeutic environment (an analytic space) and had instead begun to insert himself into the patient's life as an omnipotent object. The patient craved such an object relationship (a primitive maternal transference), but was sufficiently healthy to struggle against the enslaving addiction that such a relationship inevitably generates.

Traumatic and Nontraumatic Discovery of Separateness

In the period of the transitional phenomenon, the infant (or patient) must not be abruptly confronted with the experiential fact that he has his own mind, that he has his own area of experiencing within which he thinks his thoughts, feels his feelings, dreams his dreams, and does his playing. The infant requires time to make this experiential discovery for himself. If the infant has this opportunity, the discovery can at least in part be a welcome one (see Mahler's [1968] description of the exhilaration of the practicing subphase of separation-individuation).

The crucial psychological-interpersonal phenomenon that makes possible the weaning of the infant from the maternally provided psychological matrix is the maintenance of a series of paradoxes: The infant and mother are one, and the infant and mother are two; the infant has created the object and the object was there to be discovered; the infant must learn to be alone in the presence of the mother; and so on. It is essential that the infant or child never be asked which is the truth (Winnicott, 1951). Both are true. The simultaneous maintenance of the emotional truth of oneness with the mother and of separateness from her makes it possible for the infant to play in the potential space between mother and infant. (In Chapters 8 and 9 the normal and pathological development of potential space will be discussed.)

The experience of the absence of the mother as object is a phenomenon of the depressive position (that is, the period of development in which whole object-relatedness is being consolidated). Loss of the mother-as-object is reacted to with feelings of sadness, loneliness, guilt, and sometimes, desolation. If the capacity to be alone has been achieved (that is, if the environmental mother has been internalized), this loss can be survived. The loss of the mother-as-environment is a far more catastrophic event, to which one responds with a feeling of impending loss of oneself. The person experiences himself as on the edge of dissolving. Sometimes, if the situation has not reached a point where the patient has entered a state of panic or has instituted massive defensive withdrawal, the patient may report being unable to think or not knowing who he is.

Once when working with a patient in this state, I addressed the patient (Todd) by name. He looked at me with a combination of bewilderment, fear, and despair and said in a monotone, "Todd is lost and gone forever." The patient told me he did not know what his name was but he did not think it was Todd. He then entered a state of utter panic and fled from the office. He screamed in the hallway without words and hurled himself at the walls. It was only in the course of being held tightly in the arms of three of the ward staff that he was able to stop flailing and begin to be calmed.

As the panic mounts for a patient experiencing this form of dissolution of self, there is a powerful need to reconstruct a holding environment. It is often at this point (as in the case just described) that the patient feels compelled to create such havoc (an externalization of the internal catastrophe) that it becomes necessary for police or ward staff, physically and sometimes violently, to restrain the patient. It is essential that the containing activ-

ity be a human interaction; i.e., a person must be present
with the patient in sheets, in restraints, or in a "seclusion
room." Otherwise, the patient's terror is magnified, leaving him only suicide, profound autistic withdrawal, or self-
mutilation as methods of managing his state of psychological catastrophe. In one instance in which interpersonal
containment was not provided, it was reported to me that a
patient who had been locked in a seclusion room enu-
cleated an eye with his fingers in what was later inferred to
have been an attempt to shut out unbearable experience.

With this conception of the psychological matrix in
mind, it is now possible to reconsider aspects of Kleinian
thinking from a slightly altered perspective. For Klein,
there is an implicit notion that the matrix for the infant's
psychological life is ultimately a biological one. The life
and death instincts as vehicles for phylogenetically inherited preconceptions are together the organizer and container of psychological life. Instinctual deep structure is a
biological entity that organizes psychology and is never
directly experienced, just as one never directly experiences one's brain or one's linguistic deep structure. The
experiential manifestation of the structuring function of
the instincts is the organizing and containing effect of the
attribution of meaning (along biologically predetermined
lines) to chaotic barrages of raw sensory data. It goes
without saying that psychology is embedded in biology
(i.e., mental phenomena have physiologic substrates), but
Kleinian and Freudian instinct theory go farther than that
to implicitly offer a conception of biology (perhaps more
accurately termed psychobiology) as a matrix for a system
of psychological meanings.

For Winnicott, the infant's biological matrix inter-
penetrates the maternally provided matrix: both are unob-
trusively present unless there is a disruption of the inter-

personal matrix. When such disruptions occur, as they
inevitably do, the infant must utilize his own biologically
determined psychological defenses, including very primitive forms of splitting, projection, introjection, denial, and
idealization. From a Winnicottian perspective, these psychological operations are viewed not as defenses against
the derivatives of the death instinct, but as facets of the
infant's constitutionally given capacity to contain and
order his own experience in the face of an emergency
arising from the inevitable failure of the maternal facet of
his psychological matrix.

III. The Period of
Whole-Object Relatedness

Thus far, I have addressed the Winnicottian conception of
the role of the mother as a holding, postponing environment and the role of the mother as overseer of the weaning process through which the "internalization" (or appropriation to the infant) of the psychological matrix
occurs. I will now focus on the role of the mother in the
period of development during which the infant achieves
"unit status," i.e., whole-object relatedness in the depressive position.

The Survival of the Object and
the Discovery of Externality

In the depressive position, the infant is no longer as
dependent on the mother as matrix for his psychological
contents. He is able to provide much of that for himself.
However, his dependence on the mother has by no means
ended; it has taken on a new form. The infant is now

dependent on the mother-as-object, whom he is in the process of discovering (as opposed to creating). His continued emotional development, including the development of the capacity to "use objects" (Winnicott, 1968) and the development of psychic reality, depends upon the mother performing her role as external object over time. If we view *holding* as dominant among the functions of the mother in the earliest stage of development, and *weaning* as the dominant function in the period of the transitional phenomenon, in the depressive position[9] the critical task of the mother can be conceived of as *surviving over time*.

Here again, it is not possible to understand this aspect of Winnicott's contribution to the psychoanalytic dialogue in isolation from an understanding of the Kleinian contribution. What is being developed in this facet of Winnicott's thinking is a theory of the relationship of the infant to his internal objects, the relationship of internal objects to actual objects, and the relationship of internal objects to mental representations of external objects. In classical theory, there is no equivalent to the Kleinian conception of internal objects. For Klein, the internal object originates in the inherited preconceptions associated with the instincts (which I have referred to as psychological deep structure). The mental representation of the object is not inherited, but the structure for the idea is inherited and is given form as a mental representation when the infant encounters actual objects. The actual breast, for example, is merely a shape that is given to the

[9]The gradual attainment of the depressive position for Winnicott (1954–1955), occurs approximately in the second half of the first year of life. This development is marked by the infant's becoming able to "play at dropping things" (p. 263), an ability the infant usually develops to "a fine art" (p. 263) by about 9 months of age.

"preconception" (Bion, 1962a, 1962b) of the breast. It must be emphasized that the "preconception" is not yet a conception (an idea), but the potential for a conception, which becomes an idea when the preconception meets its "realization" (Bion, 1962a, 1962b) in the actual encounter with the breast. The infant does not anticipate the actual breast in the sense of having a mental picture of it prior to encountering it; on the other hand, he "recognizes" it when he encounters it, because it is part of his biologically structured internal order that was silently available to be given representational form.

From a Kleinian perspective, the formation of an internal object is only secondarily an internalization process. More fundamentally, this form of mental object has its origins in the infant's psychological deep structure, is given shape through the infant's experience in the world, and is then (re)internalized with the representational qualities it has accrued. Only those qualities of the actual external object that have correspondence to the structurally preconceived object are utilized ("seen") in creating the internal object representation. Representations of internal objects formed in this way stand in contrast to external object representations which are later developments. The formation of external object representations is predominantly an internalization process and depends upon the capacity of the infant to learn from experience, i.e., to notice and utilize the difference between the actual and the anticipated object. Early on, the actual object is eclipsed by the anticipated object.[10] Because internal ob-

[10]When classical analytic thinkers (e.g., Jacobson [1964] and Mahler [1968]) refer to object relations, they are predominantly referring to the real interaction with actual external objects, and the internalization that follows from this interaction. The early object is not predom-

jects are the infant's first creations, they operate almost entirely under the aegis of omnipotent thinking.

For Klein, projective identification is the principal method by which internal objects formed in the way just described are modified. The mother's containment of a projective identification is a process of modifying an infantile preconception. Through this process, internal objects are gradually "cleansed" (Grotstein, 1980a, 1980b) of projective distortion leading to the formation of external object representations. No mental representation ever entirely loses its connection with its origins as an internal object, but with adequate maternal containment of the infant's projective identifications, mental representations acquire increasing autonomy from these origins and from the omnipotent thinking associated with relations between internal objects.

This consolidation of the "externality" of the object representation is reflected in the degree to which the individual is capable of entering into relationships with actual objects in a manner that involves more than a simple transference projection of his internal object world. The schizoid patient is far more the prisoner of his omnipotent internal object world (which is projected onto current objects) than is the healthy individual, for whom transference provides only a background for relations with real objects, whose qualities are perceived and responded to even when these qualities differ from the subject's transference expectations.

---

inantly created by the infant; it is responded to, influences, and is influenced by the infant, and modifies the infant's psychological structure through an internalization process. British object relations theory (under the influence of ideas developed by Klein) places more emphasis on the role of phantasy, projection, and deep structural "anticipation" of objects.

From the perspective developed thus far, the theoretical problem for psychoanalysis is not simply to account for the creation of phantasy objects (internal objects), but also to account for the creation of external objects. In other words, psychoanalysis requires a theory that addresses the way in which the infant develops the capacity to see beyond the world he has created through the projection of internal objects.

Despite the fact that Winnicott was not satisfied with the Kleinian resolution to this theoretical problem (i.e., the notion of cleansing of internal objects through maturation and successive projective identifications), he did accept many of the basic premises out of which this theoretical problem was formulated. Specifically, he adopted the Kleinians' implicit conception of the origin of internal objects in biologically determined preconceptions, although Winnicott's conception of the specificity and nature of these preconceptions differed markedly from Klein's. For Winnicott, the infant is born with only a vague structural readiness for need-fulfilling objects. I infer that this structural readiness accounts for the way in which the infant is not surprised or excited by the object (e.g., the breast) that is empathically provided by the mother since the breast corresponds to the world the infant anticipates. Unless the object were fully "expected," i.e., fully congruent with the infant's internal order of things that predates actual experience, the infant would "notice" the object, which would result in premature awareness of separateness. It is because the infant is strucutrally (not motivationally) anticipating the object, that the object can be perceived without being noticed as separate or different from the self.

In Winnicott's conception of development, room must be made psychologically for the discovery of the external object. Winnicott (1968) states, in his enigmatic way, that it is the infant's destruction of the object (while the mother survives the destruction) that allows the infant to discover externality. What I infer he means is that the infant's renunciation of the omnipotence of the internal object entails a crucial act of faith. The infant allows himself to drop out of the arms of the omnipotent internal object,[11] into the arms of a (potential) object whom he has not yet met, since until that point the external mother has been eclipsed by the omnipotent internal-object-mother. From the point of view of an outside observer, the external-object-mother has always been there and has created (with the infant) the illusion of the subjective object. However, the very fact that this illusion has been successfully created and maintained, has allowed the infant *not to be aware of the existence of* the external-object-mother, who exists outside the realm of his omnipotence. The infant has, of course, met her but has not "noticed" her; he has mistaken her for himself (i.e., his creation). The act of faith that takes place in giving up ("destroying") the internal object is an act of trust in the (as yet invisible) presence of the external-object-mother. It is therefore crucial that the real and separate mother be there (to catch the infant) when the infant is in the process of making room for her and recognizing her through his act of renunciation (destruction) of the omnipotent internal-object-mother:

[11]For Winnicott, unconscious omnipotent internal objects are defensively created in response to painful, but inevitable disruptions of the maternal holding environment. The infant deals with the anxiety and feelings of helplessness arising from a premature awareness of separateness by constructing a world of internal objects operating according to rules reflecting his own omnipotence.

The subject says to the object [the internal object]:
"I have destroyed you," and the object [the external-
object-mother] is there to receive the communication. From now on the subject says, "Hullo, object!"
"I've destroyed you." "I love you." "You have value
for me because of your survival of my destruction of
you. While I am loving you [the real-mother-in-the-
world, outside of the infant's omnipotence], I am all
the time destroying you [the omnipotent internal-
object-mother] in (unconscious fantasy). . . . The
subject can now use the [external] object that has
survived. (Winnicott, 1968, p. 90)

The external object at this juncture can be made use
of for the first time, because the object that is being
recognized and interacted with is an object-in-the-world,
outside of oneself. Up to that point, the actual qualities of
the object, and the rootedness of the object-in-the-world
outside oneself, were imperceptible and, therefore, un-
usable. The infant had paid for his (necessary) insulation
in the illusion of the subjective object, through postponement of the discovery of a world of utilizable objects, i.e.,
people with whom he can enter into a realm of shared
experience-in-the-world outside of himself.

The survival of the object is a form of holding the
situation over time in such a way that the object-mother
(or therapist) remains emotionally present while the infant (or patient) attempts to carry out the act of trust
involved in loosening his grip on the omnipotent internal-
object-mother.

An inability to renounce the internal object arises
either when the external object fails to be there to catch
the infant when he allows himself to fall into her arms, or

when the infant's experience with the illusion of the
subjective object has not instilled in him a faith in the
world sufficient to allow him to drop into the arms of an
object he has not yet seen. When the external object fails
to survive, (i.e., fails to be physically or emotionally present when needed), the infant must tighten his hold on the
omnipotent internal object, which then becomes the only
form of safety available to the infant. The individual
becomes imprisoned in his magical internal object world to
which he then rigidly clings. As a result, he develops very
little ability to recognize or make use of the externality of
his object world.

A later version of this same process occurs when the
child allows himself or herself to leave the "orbit" of the
preoedipal mother and move into the "gravitational pull"
of the oedipal love object. The actual parental object of
oedipal love must be there to "catch the child" once he or
she has taken the risk of falling in love. When the oedipal
love object is not emotionally or physically there to recognize, accept, and (to a degree) reciprocate the child's
oedipal love, the child retreats into the orbit of the powerful preoedipal mother from whose domination he or she
may then never be able to escape.

Ruth, Guilt, and the Benign Circle

In the same psychological-interpersonal process through
which the infant discovers the externality of objects, he
also develops a dawning awareness of his impact on the
newly discovered external-object-mother. Up to this point
he has treated his mother "ruthlessly" (Winnicott, 1954–
1955), i.e., without ruth (concern). The infant has done
so, not because in his omnipotence he has wished to harm

the object, but because he has not yet developed awareness of the object as a subject, and therefore has had no empathy for the object.

The infant, in discovering the externality of objects, begins to develop a sense of how fierce he can be in his efforts to satisfy his wants and in his attempts to get rid of what gets in his way. The infant unconsciously fears that he does serious damage to his mother in the course of demanding and taking from her. The function of the mother at this point is to "hold the situation over time" (Winnicott, 1954–1955, 1968) so that the infant, while damaging the mother in (unconscious) fantasy, is at the same time discovering on a moment-to-moment basis that she is alive and present in a way that differs from his unconscious fantasy experience. It is in the simultaneous experiencing of the fantasied destruction of the internal-object-mother and the experiencing of a relationship to a mother as object who is present and unretaliative that the infant has the opportunity to juxtapose two forms of experience, both of which are real (internal and external reality). It is from this juxtaposition over time that the infant constructs the state of mind that we term psychic reality.

If, for example, the mother is able to bear with (over a period of time) the aggression involved in a vigorous feed and its sequelae, she is there, not only to survive the experience, but also to recognize the meaning of a reparative gift from the infant, and to accept the gift from him (e.g., a bowel movement or a "coo"). In this way, the mother allows the infant to make up for the fantasied harm that he has done and continues to do in fantasy, and for the strain that he has, in fact, caused.

Although Klein (1935, 1940) introduced the idea of the development in the depressive position of the wish to make reparation, she did not explore in any depth the nature of the interpersonal interaction mediating either this development or the discovery of the externality of the object. Klein was, of course, aware that the infant's feelings of guilt and his wish to make reparation are object-related phenomena. She did not, however, focus sufficient attention upon the nature of the relationship with the real external object: someone must be there to recognize the infant's feelings of guilt and to accept the infant's reparative gift if the infant's psychological act is to be brought to completion. For the completion of this "benign circle" (Winnicott, 1958a, p. 24) the infant is utterly dependent on the mother as object and cannot grow without her act of surviving the infant's fantasied destruction of her and through her unconscious recognition of the meaning and acceptance of the gift.

To recapitulate, Winnicott's conception of this third form of dependence of the infant on the mother (i.e., the dependence on the mother as object) was developed in the context of Klein's conception of internal objects and her concept of the depressive position. Winnicott differed from Klein in making central the role of the infant's experience with the mother as object. The infant's experience with an object surviving over time, in conjunction with his unconscious renunciation of the internal object, creates the conditions necessary for the discovery of the external object. This interplay of fantasy and experience with objects also generates the conditions for the creation of psychic reality, an achievement built upon the differentiation of internal and external reality. Externality is not created once and for all by a single act of "destruction" (renunciation) of the internal object. The pull of the primitive tie to the internal object must be consistently resisted. In psychological terms, the internal object must

be constantly destroyed in unconscious fantasy, thus continually making room for the rediscovery of the external
object.

Summary

In this chapter, Winnicott's conception of the development of the mother–infant into a mother and an infant
was discussed in relation to three forms of infantile dependence. The conceptualization of each of these forms of
dependence has been understood in relation to specific
aspects of the Kleinian contribution, which are both preserved and superseded in the Winnicottian contribution.

According to Winnicott, the infant in the beginning
can survive and develop only within the protective, postponing envelope of the maternal holding environment,
and in this sense, at the outset, "There is no such thing as
an infant." The unit of psychological development in the
beginning is the mother–infant. The mother's psychological and physical activity provides the initial matrix for the
infant's mental and bodily experience. The infant is protected from knowledge of separateness by the mother's
provision of the illusion of the subjective object (the
illusion that externality and internality are one and the
same).

In the period of the transitional phenomenon, the
developmental task for the mother–infant pair is the nontraumatic weaning of the infant from the maternal provision of the psychological matrix. This is achieved in part
through the infant's experience of playing alone in the
presence of the absent mother and in the absence of the
present mother. In other words, the infant must have the
experience of playing in the presence of the mother-as-

environment and in the absence of the mother-as-object. Through the internalization of the environmental mother, the infant develops the capacity to generate for himself a matrix for his psychological and bodily experience. The persistent intrusion of the mother into the infant's playing results in extreme dependence on the actual external-object-mother. This leads to the defensive internalization of the mother-as-object and an addictive relationship to an omnipotent internal-object-mother, rather than the establishment of the infant's self-generated internal holding environment (psychological matrix).

The third form of dependence is that of the infant's dependence on the mother's capacity to survive over time in the period of whole object-relatedness. The actual external-object-mother has to this point been largely eclipsed by the infant's projection of his internal object world. In the period of whole-object relatedness, the infant is engaged in the process of renouncing (in unconscious fantasy, "destroying") the omnipotent internal-object-mother, thus making room for the discovery of the actual external-object-mother. This involves an act of faith in which the infant allows himself to drop out of the arms of the omnipotent internal-object-mother into the arms of the external object who had always been there, but had never been noticed. In this process, the actual mother must be physically and emotionally present over time to survive the infant's actual and fantasied acts of destruction, and to recognize and accept his reparative gifts. The external object that is being discovered (as opposed to created) is an object that can be "used" in an entirely new way since a relationship with the discovered object is a relationship with an object rooted in the world, outside of the infant's omnipotence.

8

Potential Space

Perhaps the most important and at the same time most elusive of the ideas introduced by Donald Winnicott is the concept of potential space. *Potential space* is the general term Winnicott used to refer to an intermediate area of experiencing that lies between fantasy and reality. Specific forms of potential space include the play space, the area of the transitional object and phenomena, the analytic space, the area of cultural experience, and the area of creativity. The concept of potential space remains enigmatic in part because it has been so difficult to extricate the meaning of the concept from the elegant system of images and metaphors in which it is couched. This chapter is an attempt to clarify the concept of potential space and to explore the implications that this aspect of Winnicott's work holds for a psychoanalytic theory of the normal and pathological development of the capacity for symbolization and subjectivity.

Although potential space originates in a (potential) physical and mental space *between* mother and infant, it later becomes possible, in the course of normal development for the individual infant, child, or adult to develop his own capacity to generate potential space. This capacity constitutes an organized and organizing set of psychological activities operating in a particular mode. The concept of the dialectical process will be explored as a possible paradigm for understanding the form or mode of the psychological activity generating potential space.

Winnicott's Language

I will begin by presenting in Winnicott's words his concept of the nature of potential space. I will not attempt at this point to explicate or interpret, and for the moment will honor Winnicott's admonition to allow the paradoxes "to be accepted and tolerated and respected . . . and not to be resolved" (Winnicott, 1971e, p. xii). For Winnicott, as for perhaps no other analytic writer, it is crucial that we begin with his ideas in his own words. For Winnicott, meaning lies in the form of the writing as much as in the content: "The whole forms a unit" (Winnicott, 1967a, p. 99).

> 1. "Potential space . . . is the hypothetical area that exists (but cannot exist) between the baby and the object (mother or part of mother) during the phase of the repudiation of the object as not-me, that is, at the end of being merged in with the object." (Winnicott, 1971f, p. 107)
> 2. Playing, creativity, transitional phenomena, psychotherapy, and "cultural" experience ("the accent is on experience," 1967a, p. 99) all have a place in which they occur. That place, potential space, "is not *inside* by any use of the word. . . . Nor is it *outside*,

that is to say it is not part of the repudiated world, the not-me, that which the individual has decided to recognize (with whatever difficulty and even pain) as truly external, which is outside magical control." (1971c, p. 41). Potential space is an intermediate area of experiencing that lies between (a) the inner world, "inner psychic reality" (1971b, p. 106), and (b) "actual or external reality" (1971c, p. 41). It lies "between the subjective object and the object objectively perceived, between me-extensions and not-me" (1967a, p. 100).

3. "The essential feature [of this area of experiencing in general and the transitional object in particular] is . . . *the paradox and the acceptance of the paradox*: the baby creates the object, but the object was there waiting to be created. . . . In the rules of the game we all know that we will never challenge the baby to elicit an answer to the question: did you create that or did you find it?" (1968, p. 89).

4. This "area is a product of the *experiences of the individual person* (baby, child, adolescent, adult) in the environment that obtains." (1971b, p. 107)

5. Potential space both joins and separates the infant (child, or adult) and the mother (object). "This is the paradox I accept and do not attempt to resolve. The baby's separating-out of the world of objects from the self is achieved only through the absence of a space between [the infant and mother], the *potential* space being filled in in the way that I am describing" [i.e., with illusion, with playing and with symbols]. (1971b, p. 108)

It seems to me that within the framework of the metaphors and paradoxes that Winnicott has generated to convey his conception of potential space, there is little if anything I can add to clarify or extend what he has said. It is very difficult to find words of one's own to discuss the extremely complex set of ideas that Winnicott has managed to condense into his deceptively simple, highly evocative metaphorical language. Winnicott's ideas are entrapped, to a far greater degree than is ordinarily the case, in the language in which they are presented. The result is a peculiar combination of clarity and opacity in Winnicott's thinking about potential space that has given it popular appeal (the concept of the transitional object in particular) while at the same time insulating the ideas from systematic exploration, modification, and extension.

It is one of the tasks of this chapter to use language not used by Winnicott to discuss the phenomena addressed by the concept of potential space. The new terms, it is hoped, will not alter the essential meanings of the original language and may provide access to understandings of potential space not provided by Winnicott.

The Phenomenon of Playing

It might be useful at this point to present some of the experiential referents for the abstract set of ideas involved in the concept of potential space. In the following example, the state of mind required for playing (i.e., potential space) is at first absent and then made present.

A two-and-a-half-year-old child, after having been frightened by having his head go underwater while being given a bath, became highly resistant to taking a bath. Some months later, after gentle but persistent coaxing by his mother, he very reluctantly allowed himself to be placed in four inches of bath water. The child's entire body was tense; his hands were tightly clamped onto his mother's. He was not crying, but his eyes were pleadingly glued to those of his mother. One knee was locked in extension while the other was flexed in order to hold as much of himself out of the water as he could. His mother began almost immediately to try to interest him in some bath toys. He was not the least bit interested until she told him she would like some tea. At that point the tension that had been apparent in his arms, legs, abdomen, and particularly his face, abruptly gave way to a new physical and psychological state. His knees were now bent a little; his eyes surveyed the toy cups and saucers and spotted an empty shampoo bottle, which he chose to use as milk for the tea; the tension in his voice shifted from the tense insistent plea, "My not like bath, my not like bath," to a narrative of his play: "Tea not too hot, it's okay now. My blow on it for you. Tea yummy." The mother has some "tea" and asked for more. After a few minutes, the mother began to reach for the washcloth. This resulted in the child's ending of the play as abruptly as he had started it, with a return of all of the initial signs of anxiety that had preceded the play. After the mother reassured the child that she would hold him so he would not slip, she asked him if he had any more tea. He did, and playing was resumed.

The foregoing is observational data and does not emanate from a psychoanalytic process. Nonetheless, the observations do convey a sense of the way in which a state of mind was generated by the mother and child in which there was a transformation of water from something frightening to a plastic medium (discovered and created by the child) with meanings that could be communicated. In this transformation, reality is not denied; the dangerous water is represented in the playing. Nor is fantasy robbed of its vitality—the child's breath magically changed dangerous water into a loving gift. There is also a quality of "I-ness" that is generated in play that differs from the riveted stare and desperate holding-on that had connected mother and infant prior to the beginning of play. In the course of this chapter the significance of each of the features of the state of mind noted here will be discussed.

Potential Space and the Dialectical Process

A dialectic is a process in which each of two opposing concepts creates, informs, preserves, and negates the other, each standing in a dynamic (ever-changing) relationship with the other (Hegel, 1807; Kojève, 1934–1935). The dialectical process moves toward integration, but integration is never complete. Each integration creates a new dialectical opposition and a new dynamic tension. In psychoanalysis, the central dialectic is that of Freud's conception of the relationship between the conscious and the unconscious mind. There can be no conscious mind without an unconscious mind and vice versa; each creates the other and exists only as a hypothetical possibility without the other. In mathematical language, the conscious mind and unconscious mind independent of one another are empty sets; they become full only in relation to one another. The unconscious mind acquires psychological contents only to the extent that there is a category of psychological event that has the quality of consciousness and vice versa.

The dialectical process is centrally involved in the creation of subjectivity. By subjectivity, I am referring to the capacity for degrees of self-awareness ranging from intentional self-reflection (a very late achievement) to the most subtle, unobtrusive sense of "I-ness" by which experience is subtly endowed with the quality that one is thinking one's thoughts and feeling one's feelings as opposed to living in a state of reflexive reactivity. Subjectivity is related to, but not the same as, consciousness. The experience of consciousness (and unconsciousness) follows from the achievement of subjectivity. Subjectivity, as will be discussed, is a reflection of the differentiation of symbol, symbolized, and interpreting subject. The emergence of a subject in the course of this differentiation makes it possible for a person to wish. The wish to make oneself unaware of an aspect of one's system of meanings sets the stage for the differentiation of conscious and unconscious realms of experience.

Paradoxically, "I-ness" is made possible by the other. Winnicott (1967b) describes this as the infant's discovery of himself in what he sees reflected in his mother's eyes. This constitutes an interpersonal dialectic wherein 'I-ness" and otherness create one another and are preserved by the other. The mother creates the infant and the infant creates the mother. (In discussing dialectics, we are always considering concepts [e.g., the concept of mother and the concept of infant] and not material entities.)

Meaning accrues from difference. There can be no meaning in a completely homogeneous field. The existence of the homogeneous field itself could not even be recognized, because there would be no terms other than itself to attribute to it. One cannot have a dictionary with only one word; in theory, one can have a dictionary with two words, because each word would supply the contrast necessary for the recognition and definition of the other. From this perspective, the unconscious mind *in itself* does

not constitute a system of meanings. There are no negatives and no contradictions in the unconscious (Freud,
1915b), simply the static coexistence of opposites that is
the hallmark of primary process thinking. The system
Conscious is required to generate unconscious *meaning*
and the system Unconscious is required to create conscious
meaning.

At the very beginning (perhaps only a hypothetical
moment), the subjectivity of the mother–infant unit is
only a potential held by the aspect of the mother that lies
outside of the mother–infant. Winnicott (1960a) can be
taken quite literally when he says that there is no such
thing as an infant (without a mother). I would add that
within the mother–infant unit, neither is there any such
thing as a mother. The preoccupation of the mother (what
an observer would see as the mother) with fitting herself
into the place of the infant would be considered an illness
if this type of loss of oneself in another were to occur in a
different setting (Winnicott, 1956).

The mother–infant (in isolation from the part of the
mother that is outside this unity) is incapable of subjectivity. Instead, there is the "illusion"[1] (in most ways closer

---

[1]The term *illusion* is used at different points by Winnicott to refer to
two quite dissimilar phenomena. The first is the illusion of the
subjective object (more accurately described as the illusion of the
invisible subject and object), where the mother's empathic respon-
siveness protects the infant from premature awareness of the self and
of the other. This illusion provides a protective insulation for the
infant (Winnicott, 1948).

The second (developmentally later) form of illusion is the illusion that fills potential space, e.g., the form of illusion encountered in
playing. Here, the experience of oneness with the mother and separateness from her coexist in a dialectical opposition (Winnicott,
1971c).

to a delusion) that the mother and infant are not separate and in fact do not exist. The mother exists only in the form of the invisible holding environment in which there is a meeting of the infant's needs in a way that is so unobtrusive that the infant does not experience his needs as needs. As a result, there is not yet an infant.

If there is a good-enough fit between mother and infant and such an illusion/delusion is created, there is no need for symbols, even of the most primitive type. Instead, there is an undisturbed state of "going on being" (Winnicott, 1956, p. 303) that will later become the background of experience, but at present is invisible because there is nothing with which to contrast it; it is both background and foreground. Symbols are required only when there is desire; at the stage of development being discussed, there is only need that is met; the satisfied need does not generate desire (i.e., wishing) for which symbols are required.

The undisturbed, harmoniously functioning mother–infant unit may be only a hypothetical entity, because of the inevitable imperfection of fit between mother and infant.[2] The well-dosed frustration that results provides the first opportunity for awareness of separateness.

At this point, the task for the aspect of the mother

[2]The research findings of Brazelton (Brazelton and Als, 1979), Sander (1964), Stern (1977), and others reveals an active "dialogue" between mother and infant from the first days of life. This suggests the possibility of an early, nontraumatic sensing of otherness. Grotstein (1981) has pointed out that it is not necessary to decide if there is mother–infant unity or if there is early awareness of otherness. The two may coexist as separate "tracks" of a dual consciousness. (The need for developmental thinking to include both synchronic and diachronic axes was discussed in Chapter 7.)

who is not a part of the mother–infant unit is to make her presence (the mother as object) known in a way that is not frightening and therefore does not have to be denied or in other ways defended against by the infant. It is this period of the very earliest awareness of separateness, beginning at "about four to six to eight to twelve months" (Winnicott, 1951, p. 4), that has been the focus of Winnicott's work on potential space. He has proposed that, in order for this transition from mother–infant unity to a state in which there is mother-and-infant to be nonpathogenic, there must be a potential space between mother and infant that is always potential (never actual) because it is filled in with the state of mind that embodies the never-challenged paradox: The infant and mother are one, and the infant and mother are two.

The movement from mother–infant unity (invisible environmental mother) to mother and infant (mother as object) requires the establishment of the capacity for a psychological dialectic of oneness and of separateness in which each creates and informs the other. At first the "twoness" (that coexists with oneness) cannot be distributed between the mother and the infant in a way that clearly demarcates the two as separate individuals; rather, at this point twoness is a quality of the mother–infant. This is what Winnicott (1958a) is referring to when he talks about the infant's development of the capacity to be alone in the presence of the mother. The transitional object is a symbol for this separateness in unity, unity in separateness. The transitional object is at the same time the infant (the omnipotently created extension of himself) and not the infant (an object he has discovered that is outside of his omnipotent control).

The appearance of a relationship with a transitional

object is not simply a milestone in the process of separa-tion–individuation. The relationship with the transitional object is as significantly a reflection of the development of the capacity to maintain a psychological dialectical pro-cess.

The consequences of this achievement are momen-tous and include the capacity to generate personal mean-ings represented in symbols that are mediated by subjec-tivity (the experience of oneself as subject who has created one's symbols). The attainment of the capacity to maintain psychological dialectics involves the transforma-tion of the unity that did not require symbols into "three-ness," a dynamic interplay of three differentiated entities. These entities are the symbol (a thought), the symbolized (that which is being thought about), and the interpreting subject (the thinker generating his own thoughts and interpreting his own symbols). For heuristic purposes, the original homogeneity of the mother–infant unit can be thought of as a point (Grotstein, 1978). The differentia-tion of symbol, symbolized, and interpreting subject creates the possibility of triangularity within which space is created. That space between symbol and symbolized, mediated by an interpreting self, is the space in which creativity becomes possible and is the space in which we are alive as human beings, as opposed to being simply reflexively reactive beings. This is Winnicott's potential space.

This transformation of unity into threeness coincides with the transformation of the mother–infant unit into mother, infant, and observer of mother-and-infant as three distinct entities. Oneness (the invisible mother–infant) becomes threeness, since at the moment of differ-entiation within the mother–infant unit, not only are the mother and infant created as objects, but also, the infant is created as subject. The infant as subject is the observer of mother and infant as (symbolic) objects; the infant is now the creator and interpreter of his symbols.

Psychopathology of Potential Space

Winnicott states that symbols originate within potential space. In the absence of potential space, there is only fantasy; within potential space imagination can develop. In fantasy, "a dog is a dog is a dog" (1971d, p. 33), while imagination involves a layering of symbolic meanings. In these very brief statements, Winnicott points to a theory of the psychopathology of the symbolic function, a theory that remains to be completed. In this section, I will attempt to begin to fill in that theory of the psychopathology of symbolization by studying various forms of incompleteness or collapse of the capacity to maintain a psychological dialectical process. As will be seen, the symbolic function is a direct consequence of the capacity to maintain psychological dialectics, and the psychopathology of symbolization is based on specific forms of failure to create or maintain these dialectics.

As was discussed earlier, when there is a good-enough fit between mother and infant, in the very beginning (in the period of the invisible mother–infant), there is no need or opportunity for symbols. Within the context of the mother–infant unit, the person whom an observer would see as the mother is invisible to the infant and exists only in the fulfillment of need that the infant does not yet recognize as need. The mother–infant unity can be disrupted by the mother's substitution of something of herself for the infant's spontaneous gesture. Winnicott

(1952) refers to this as "impingement." Some degree of failure of empathy is inevitable and in fact essential for the infant to come to recognize needs as wishes. However, there comes a point at which repeated impingement constitutes "cumulative trauma" (Khan, 1963; Ogden, 1978).

Cumulative trauma is at one pole of a wide spectrum of causes of premature disruption of the mother–infant unity. Other causes include constitutional hypersensitivity (of many types) on the part of the infant, trauma resulting from physical illness of the infant, and illness or death of a parent or sibling. When premature disruption of the mother–infant unity occurs for any reason, several distinct forms of failure to create or adequately maintain the psychological dialectical process may result:

1. The dialectic of reality and fantasy collapses in the direction of fantasy (i.e., reality is subsumed by fantasy) so that fantasy becomes a thing in itself as tangible, as powerful, as dangerous and as gratifying as the external reality from which it cannot be differentiated.

2. The dialectic of reality and fantasy may become limited or collapse in the direction of reality when reality is used predominantly as a defense against fantasy. Under such circumstances, reality robs fantasy of its vitality. Imagination is foreclosed.

3. The dialectic of reality and fantasy becomes restricted when reality and fantasy are dissociated in such a way as to avoid a specific set of meanings, e.g., the "splitting of the ego" in fetishism.

4. When the mother and infant encounter serious and sustained difficulty in being a mother–infant, the infant's premature and traumatic awareness of his separateness makes experience so unbear-

able that extreme defensive measures are instituted that take the form of a cessation of the attribution of meaning to perception. Experience is foreclosed. It is not so much that fantasy or reality is denied; rather, neither is created.

These four categories are meant only as examples of types of limitation of the dialectical process. In no sense is this list meant to be exhaustive.

Reality Subsumed by Fantasy

The first of the forms of failure to create and maintain a psychological dialectical process is that in which the "reality pole" of the psychological dialectic is not established on an equal plane with the "fantasy pole" or is weakened by actual experience that is felt to be indistinguishable from, and therefore powerfully confirmatory of, fantasy. The term *reality* is not used to denote something independent of one's processing of perception, since even at our most "realistic," we organize, and in that sense create, our perceptions according to our individual psychological schemata. The term *reality* is used here to refer to that which is experienced as outside of the realm of the subject's omnipotence.

When the "reality pole" of the psychological dialectic collapses, the subject becomes tightly imprisoned in the realm of fantasy objects as things in themselves. This is a two-dimensional world which is experienced as a collection of facts. The hallucination does not sound like a voice, it *is* a voice. One's husband does not simply behave coldly, he *is* ice. One does not feel like one's father, one's father *is* in one's blood and must be bled out in order for one to be free of him. The form of transference generated when the psychological dialectic of reality and fantasy has collapsed in the direction of fantasy is the delusional transference (see Little, 1958; Searles, 1963): the therapist is not like the patient's mother, he *is* the patient's mother.

A borderline patient experiencing the form of collapse of potential space under discussion became terrified of department store mannequins, feeling that they were living people. For this patient there was no concept of mannequins being "life-like"; either they were alive or they were not. One thing does not stand for another. Things are what they are. (Segal [1957] uses the term *symbolic equation* for this relationship of symbol and symbolized.)

As one approaches the state where nothing is felt to represent anything but itself, one becomes more and more imprisoned in the realm of the thing in itself. Little that one experiences can be *understood*, because understanding involves a system of layering of meanings, one layer forming the context by which the other layers take on significance. For example, the past, the present, dreams, and transference experiences, each provides a context for the understanding of the others and is understandable only in terms of the others.

With limited capacity to distinguish symbol and symbolized, that which is perceived is unmediated by subjectivity (a sense of oneself as creator of meanings). The upshot is that perceptions carry with them an impersonal imperative for action and must be gotten rid of, clung to, concealed, hidden from, put into someone else, worshipped, shattered, etc. What the person cannot do is understand. This is so, not because the person does not

wish to understand his experience; rather it is so because
as one approaches the realm of the thing in itself, everything is what it is, so that the potential for understanding
simply does not exist.

A borderline patient *knew* that the therapist, who had
begun the hour three minutes late, did so because he
preferred the patient whose hour preceded this patient's. The patient told the therapist that she had
decided to terminate therapy, something she had
been thinking about doing for a long time but had not
previously told the therapist. Attempts on the part of
the therapist to understand why the patient interpreted the lateness in this particular way were met
with exasperation. The patient accused the therapist
of relying on textbook interpretations to deny the
obvious.

For this patient, feelings are facts to be acted upon
and not emotional responses to be understood. There is no
space between symbolized (the therapist's lateness) and
the symbol (the patient's emotionally colored representation of the therapist). The two (the interpretation and the
external event) are treated as one. A patient recently told
me, "You can't tell me I don't see what I see." With the
collapse of the distinction between symbol and symbolized, there is no room in which to "entertain" ideas and
feelings. Transference takes on a deadly serious quality;
illusion becomes delusion; thoughts become plans; feelings become impending actions; transference projections
become projective identifications; play becomes compulsion.
Understanding the meaning of one's experience is
possible only when one thing can stand for another with-

out being the other; this is what constitutes the attainment of the capacity for symbol formation proper (Segal, 1957). The development of the capacity for symbol formation proper frees one from the prison of the realm of the thing in itself.[3]

Reality as Defense against Fantasy

A second form of pathological distortion of the psychological dialectical process is that in which "the reality pole" of the dialectical process is used predominantly as a defense against fantasy. Whenever the potential for a psychological dialectical process is limited for defensive purposes (i.e., to exclude, modify, or diminish the significance of a given group of possible thoughts), a price is paid. In this case, the price is the foreclosure of imagination.

When a relatively unrestricted psychological dialectical process has been established, a little girl playing house is both a little girl and a mother, and the question of which she is, never arises. Being a little girl who feels loved by her mother (*in reality*) makes it safe for her to borrow what is her mother's (*in fantasy*) without fear of retaliation or fear of losing herself in her mother, and, as a result, disappearing as a separate person. Being a mother (*in fantasy*) gives the little girl access to and use of all the richness of the cultural, familial, and personal symbols

---

[3]Lacan (1949–1960) has pointed out that the individual, having attained the capacity for symbolization, becomes freed of one form of imprisonment (that of unmediated sensory experience) only to enter a new prison, that of the symbolic order. In the realm of the symbolic order, language provides us with symbols that long preexisted us and in that way determines our thoughts, even though we labor under the illusion that we create our own symbols.

(e.g., in relation to what it means to be a female, a mother, and a daughter) that have been consciously and unconsciously conveyed in the course of *real* experience with her mother, father, and others.

On the other hand, if the little girl is *only* a little girl, she is unable to play; she is unable to imagine and will be unable to feel she is alive in any full sense. Such a situation arises when reality must be used as a defense against fantasy.[4]

A boy who had been allowed to witness his parents having intercourse, as well as the very painful delivery of his younger brother, had developed by the age of 6 a precocious intelligence and a "grown-up" mode of relating that was marked by a profound skepticism. He was interested in finding "logical" explanations for "amazing" things, in particular, television stunts. When as a 7 year old he was taken to a marionette show, his parents became concerned because the boy found nothing pleasurable about the show and instead was preoccupied by his awareness of the fact that the characters were only wooden, carved figures dangling on strings that were manipulated by people behind the screen. Of course, his perception was "accurate," but the powerful awareness of this reality prevented the dialectical interplay of fantasy and reality that generates the possibility for imagination. For this child, the danger of wishes and fears "com-

---

[4]If the little girl is *only* a mother, she is psychotic and will in time become terrified by her fantasied posession of adult sexuality and adult (omnipotent) power over life and death. Here, the reality pole of the dialectic has collapsed into the fantasy pole of the dialectic as discussed earlier.

ing true" in a destructive and terribly frightening way had in all likelihood been made too real by his interpretation of what he had witnessed ("behind the scenes") earlier in his life. Such dramatic early experiences are neither a necessary nor a sufficient condition for fantasies to be experienced as frightening things that need to be controlled through an exaggerated appeal to reality.

Patients chronically experiencing this form of collapse of the dialectical process present few if any dreams, dismissing the ones they do present as "senseless," "crazy," "stupid," "weird," and the like. When dreams are presented by these patients, the dreams are often barely distinguishable from their conscious thoughts, e.g., the dreams may depict embarrassing situations that the patient regularly thinks about consciously. Associations to the dreams are often a cataloging of which parts of the dream did or did not "really" occur and precisely what the real situation was that is alluded to or depicted in the dream.

Some of these patients are keen observers and will notice when a single book has been moved in a large bookshelf in the therapist's office. When the patient is asked about his response to a detail that has been noticed, the patient will be extremely skeptical about what benefit could possibly accrue from a discussion of such a trivial thing. I have been told at such moments that looking for some personal significance in the observed detail would be "like trying to get blood from a stone." The fixity of the patient's focus on reality is in fact designed to "drain the blood out" of fantasy. The dialectical resonance of realistic and fantastic meanings is foreclosed, leaving the patient incapable of imagination.

Dissociation of Reality and Fantasy

Fetishes and perversions can be understood as representing a particular form of limitation of the dialectical process in which the reality and fantasy poles become dissociated from one another. Freud (1927) pointed out that
fetishes involve a "splitting of the ego" in such a way that
the subject both knows and does not know that women do
not have penises. This psychological state does not constitute a true psychological dialectic, because it has been
constructed largely in the service of denial and as a result
involves a severe limitation of the way in which one pole
of the dialectic is allowed to inform and be informed by
the other. A dialectical process becomes limited when one
imposes restrictions upon it: all possible combinations of
meanings are possible except those leading to the thought
that women do not have penises. That thought, or any
derivative of it, must never be thought. To the extent that
there is such a limitation placed on a dialectical process,
reality and fantasy no longer inform one another and
instead stand isolated in a state of static coexistence. A
dialectical relationship allows for resonance of meanings,
for example, conscious and unconscious meanings. Splitting of the type involved in perversions and fetishism can
be understood as involving not only denial, but also the
foreclosure of dialectical resonance that might generate
meanings that one feels are dangerous.

Foreclosure of Reality and Fantasy

The final form of failure to achieve the capacity to create
and maintain a psychological dialectical process that will
be addressed is more extreme than those discussed thus
far. The forms of dysfunction described previously have

all involved a limitation of (metaphorically, a "collapse" of) a dialectic that had to a significant degree been established and was secondarily becoming limited. What will be discussed now is a primary failure to generate a psychological dialectical process manifesting itself as a "state of nonexperience" (Ogden, 1980). In a state of nonexperience there is perception, but perception remains raw sensory data that is not attributed meaning. Meanings are not denied, they simply are not created. This state has been described variously as a "foreclosure" of the psychological (McDougall, 1974), as an "absence" analogous to that seen in a petit mal seizure (Meltzer, 1975), as "blank psychosis" (Green, 1975), psychotic "not-being" (Grotstein, 1979b), and as "death in life" (Laing, 1959). In the context of intensive psychotherapeutic work with chronic schizophrenic patients, I have described the state of nonexperience as a state in which

> . . . all experience is emotionally equivalent, one thing is just as good or just as bad as anything else; all things, people, places and behavior are emotionally interchangeable. . . . Everything can be substituted for everything else, creating a situation analogous to a numerical system in which there are an infinite number of integers but all are equal to one another in value. Addition, subtraction and all other operations would be formally possible, but there would be no point in any of them, since you would always arrive at the same value with which you had begun. (Ogden, 1980, p. 520)

As I have discussed elsewhere (Ogden, 1980, 1982a, 1982b), I view the state of nonexperience as a superordinate defense resorted to when all other defensive opera-

tions have proved insufficient to protect the infant against
sustained, overwhelming psychological pain. Under such
circumstances the infant ceases to attribute meaning to
his perception, thus failing to generate emotional significance (personal meaning) of any type. In the context of
the present discussion, this amounts to the foreclosure of
the possibility of generating both realistic and fantastic
meanings, thus denying the infant the elements from
which he might construct a dialectical process involving
fantasy and reality.

The Symbol, the Symbolized, and Subjectivity

As has been discussed, the establishment of the psychological dialectical process creates conditions wherein experience is attributed meanings that can be understood as
opposed to simply constituting a pattern of facts to be
acted upon. The establishment of the distinction between
the symbol and the symbolized is inseparable from the
establishment of subjectivity: the two achievements are
two facets of the same developmental event. Paraphrasing
Winnicott, one could say that potential space lies between
the symbol and the symbolized. To distinguish symbol
from symbolized is to distinguish one's thought from that
which one is thinking about, one's feeling from that which
one is responding to. For symbol to stand independently of
symbolized, there must be a subject engaged in the process
of interpreting perceptions. One might ask what is new in
this supposed developmental advance, because logically
there has always been a person interpreting his experience. That is, of course, so from an outside observer's
point of view, but it has not been so from the subject's

point of view. In fact, a subject did not exist when symbol and symbolized were undifferentiable.

The achievement of the capacity to distinguish symbol and symbolized is the achievement of subjectivity.[5] From this point on, symbolic function always involves the threeness of the interrelationship of three distinct entities: (1) the symbol (the thought); (2) the symbolized (that which is being thought about); and (3) the thinker (the interpreting self), who is creating his thoughts and who stands apart from both the thought and the thing being thought about. Potential space ceases to exist as any two of these three elements become dedifferentiated: the thinker and the symbol, the symbol and the symbolized, or the thinker and the object of thought (the symbolized).

There are important implications in the foregoing discussion for a theory of the development of the capacity for symbolization. The period prior to the establishment of the dialectical process (prior to the period of the transitional phenomenon) is characterized not by internal objects as things in themselves, as Melanie Klein (1946) would have it, but, rather, by an absence of the need for symbols at all. In the period of the "invisible" mother–infant unit there is neither a mother nor an infant since the environmental mother exists only as the invisible fulfillment of the infant's needs before they become desires.

As discussed earlier, Winnicott's conception of development can be thought of as a movement from an original state of "oneness" that is not experienced as oneness because the homogeneity of the situation precludes an appreciation of difference and, therefore, the delineation

[5]This parallels the Kleinian conception of the creation of psychic reality in the depressive position (Klein, 1958).

of meanings. The developmental progression, in the context of good-enough mothering, is to "threeness," wherein there is a relationship between symbol and symbolized that is mediated by an interpreting subject. The invisible mother–infant has become a mother-and-infant as (symbolic) objects, and infant as interpreting subject. The infant as subject makes it possible for the infant to become aware of the mother's subjectivity. This then allows for the development of "ruth" (Winnicott, 1958b), the capacity for concern for another person as a whole and separate human being capable of feelings *like*, not the same as, one's own. With the development of this awareness of the subjectivity of the other comes the capacity for guilt, for mourning, for empathy, and for the desire to make reparations as opposed to magical restoration of the damaged object.

From this perspective, the breakdown of the dialectical process generating the realm of the thing in itself can be understood to have a specific place in the development of object relations: twoness (infant and mother as objects in the absence of infant as interpreting subject) corresponds to the realm of the thing in itself. There are only objects and no subjects. This is always a product of the breakdown of threeness (the dialectic of fantasy and reality, symbol and symbolized mediated by a subject) and not the normative progression from the invisible oneness of the original mother–infant unit.

Winnicott thus implies that he views the normal development of fantasy as being from its inception part of a dialectical process in which fantasy creates and is created by reality. Such a conclusion runs counter to Melanie Klein's (1946, 1952c) notion of the place in normal development of the paranoid–schizoid position prior to the depressive position. In the paranoid–schizoid posi-

tion, fantasy, symbolic equation, and part–object relatedness predominate. For Klein the depressive position
(threeness consisting of subject, symbol and symbolized)
develops out of the twoness of the paranoid-schizoid position (symbol and symbolized in the absence of a subject
capable of awareness of psychic reality.) For Winnicott,
the form of fantasy that Klein associates with the paranoid-schizoid position (a form of fantasy using symbolic
equation as the mode of symbolization) always represents
a breakdown of threeness. There are inevitable break-
downs in the development of threeness because of inevitable and necessary failures in the mother–infant relationship. This leads the infant to defend himself psychologically in a paranoid-schizoid mode. Pathological development ensues only when the failures in the mother–
infant relationship (leading to the breakdown of threeness) are extreme or chronic.

Empathy and Projective Identification

The foregoing discussion of the development of the dialectical process and symbolization provides a context for an
enhanced understanding of aspects of projective identification and its relationship to empathy.

Empathy is a psychological process (as well as a form
of object-relatedness) that occurs within the context of a
dialectic of being and not-being the other. Within this
context, (Winnicott would say, "within potential space"),
one plays with the idea of being the other while knowing
that one is not. It is possible to try on for size one
identification and then another (i.e., to play with the
feeling of being the other in different ways), because the
opposite pole of the dialectic diminishes the danger of

being trapped in the other and ultimately of losing oneself in the other. Projective identification, on the other hand, can be understood as a psychological-interpersonal process (a form of defense, communication, and object-relatedness) occurring outside of the dialectic of being and not-being the other, i.e., outside of potential space.

Projective identification can be thought of as involving the following components or "phases" (Ogden, 1979, 1982a): (1) an unconscious projective fantasy of depositing a part of oneself in the other, (2) an interpersonal pressure exerted on the other to experience himself and behave in congruence with the unconscious projective fantasy, and (3) the "recipient's" processing of the induced experience followed by the projector's reinternalizing (by means of introjection or identification) of a modified version of that aspect of himself that had been (in fantasy) ejected.

Interpersonally, projective identification is the negative of playing; it is a coercive enlistment of another person to perform a role in the projector's externalized unconscious fantasy. The effect of this process on the recipient is to threaten his ability to experience his subjective state as psychic reality. Instead, his perceptions are experienced as "reality" as opposed to a personal construction. This process represents a limitation of the recipient's psychological dialectical processes by which symbolic meanings are generated and understood. Neither the projector nor the recipient of the projective identification is able to experience a range of personal meanings. On the contrary, there is only a powerful sense of inevitability. Neither party can conceive of himself or of the other, any differently or less intensely than he does at present (Ogden, 1981).

The "processing" of a projective identification by a therapist can be understood as the therapist's act of re-establishing a psychological dialectical process in which the induced feeling state can be experienced, thought about, and understood by an interpreting subject. This dialectical process has both intrapsychic and interpersonal dimensions. That is, both subjectivity and intersubjectivity are involved. The set of meanings generated in this process provides the data with which the therapist might develop an understanding of the transference, instead of feeling compelled to act upon, deny, or accept the inevitability of his current experience of himself and of the patient.

I was asked to consult on a patient diagnosed as borderline who had been hospitalized for a few days after a suicide gesture. A male member of the nursing staff who had been working with this patient told me that the patient was extremely competitive, to the point that it was nearly impossible to engage in any kind of ward activity with her. The previous evening, he had seen the patient with a deck of playing cards and had asked her if she wanted to have a game of cards. The patient agreed, but immediately proceeded to shower him with criticism about the way he shuffled and dealt the cards. The nurse told me that he explained to the patient that he had no desire to enter into a struggle with her and that when she wanted to play cards, he would be happy to do so if she would let him know. He then walked away, and the patient did not approach him after that.

When I spoke with the patient for the consultation, she said that she was nervous about talking with me and when I inquired why, she said she was afraid she would not do well at it. When I asked her in what way she was afraid of failing, she told me that she was concerned that she would be less than honest—not that she would be dishonest in the sense of lying, but that she would leave me with a false impression of her. In the course of the interview, she told me a number of things about herself, all of which, I later found out from her therapist, were interpretations he had given her. The interview had a routine feeling to it, very much that of a patient talking to a doctor. There was almost no sense of discovery, surprise, humor, or originality on either of our parts. I could not shake the awareness that we were sitting in a room in a hospital and that I was a psychiatrist conducting an interview with a patient. As a result, it felt as if nothing spontaneous could happen between us. The patient fed me the insights that she thought I wanted from her, but she was not depleted or robbed in the process because the insights were not hers and she did not value them. They were hospital property given to her by another doctor, and she was merely passing them on to me.

Something else was occurring between the patient and me that I was only subliminally aware of during the interview, but which became clearer immediately after the interview was over. When I left the meeting with this patient, I felt a pressing need to talk to someone. It did not have to be anyone in particular or about any specific topic, but the need to talk with someone was unmistakable. It took some time for me to become aware of the loneliness I had felt while talking to this patient.

As I thought about the interview with this patient, her behavior with the nurse the previous evening made more sense. She had ridiculed the way he was playing, not in order to defeat him, but to hide from him and from herself the fact that she did not know how to play. Of course, she knew the rules of the game, but she could not enter into a frame of mind in which playing might take place. Similarly, with me she began the interview by warning me that our talk might look like a meaningful exchange, but it would not be one. (I am referring to her anxiety about the false impression she would give me.) What would look like discoveries about herself would prove to be only stale repetitions of her therapist's ideas. Her principal communication to the nurse and to me was a plea for us to understand that she felt intensely isolated by her inability to play. Her communication was not in words, but by means of an induction of a feeling of loneliness in me. This is what Winnicott would call a "direct communication" (1971d, p. 54), and what I would understand as a projective identification. When a patient is incapable of generating the state of mind necessary for playing to occur, he or she will be isolated from others except by means of the direct kind of linkage possible in projective identification. "Only in playing is communication possible, except direct communication which belongs to psychopathology or to an extreme of immaturity" (Winnicott, 1971d, p. 54).

Summary

I have proposed that Winnicott's concept of potential space be understood as a state of mind based upon a series of dialectical relationships between fantasy and reality, me and not-me, symbol and symbolized, etc., each pole of the dialectic creating, informing, and negating the other. The achievement of such a dialectical process occurs by means of a developmental advance from the "invisible oneness" of the mother–infant unit to the subjective threeness of the mother-and-infant (as symbolic objects) and the infant (as interpreting subject). Failure to create or maintain the dialectical process leads to specific forms of psychopathology that include the experience of the fantasy object as a thing in itself, the defensive use of reality that forecloses imagination, the relationship to a fetish object, and the state of "nonexperience." The "processing" of a projective identification is understood as the reestablishment of the recipient's capacity to maintain a dialectical process (e.g., of me and not-me) that had been limited in the course of the recipient's unconscious participation in the projector's externalized, unconscious fantasy.

9

Dream Space and Analytic Space

In this chapter, aspects of two forms of potential space will be considered: dream space and analytic space. Dreaming is understood as an internal communication in which a dream presentation is generated by one aspect of self and understood by another aspect of self. The dream presentation as thing in itself is brought into a dialectical process by another aspect of self through which process symbolic meanings and dream experience are generated. The schizophrenic, when unable to maintain a psychological dialectical process, transforms the dream presentation into a hallucination.

The analytic space is viewed as an intersubjective state, generated by patient and therapist, in which meanings can be played with, considered, understood, etc. The patient's projective identification is a "direct" form of communication that undermines the therapist's capacity to maintain a psychological dialectical process. The therapist undermines the analytic space when his interventions

233

constitute "statements of facts." The latter contribute to a foreclosure of the realm of personal meanings and experience.

Dream Space

Up until the time that Donald Winnicott introduced his work on potential space, psychoanalysis had developed a rather full knowledge of dream construction and symbolism, but a very incomplete understanding of dreaming. In this chapter, I will propose that the dream presentation must undergo a transformation in a "dream space" in order for dreaming to occur. This is an extension of Winnicott's distinction between fantasy and imagination: the former is a static, dissociated process that remains isolated from living and dreaming (1971b, p. 27). Imagination represents the result of a transformation that fantasy undergoes when it is brought into potential space, i.e., when there is "a place from which to become aware" (1971b, p. 27 fn.) of one's fantasies. Before there is such a place (potential space), a fantasy object is a static thing in itself, devoid of resonating symbolic meanings, representing nothing but itself: in fantasy "a dog is a dog is a dog" (1971b, p. 33).

A dream will be viewed here as an internal communication involving a primary process construction generated by one aspect of self that must be *perceived, understood,* and *experienced* by another aspect of self. The primary process construction constitutes the dream presentation which is an internal sensory event. As with every other sensory registration (including communications from other people), the dream presentation initially constitutes a thing in itself from the point of view of the aspect of self attempting to understand it. This raw sensory data must undergo some form of psychological transformation in order for dreaming to occur.

Grotstein (1979b) makes a similar distinction between the dream presentation and dreaming when he differentiates the dreamer-who-dreams-the-dream from the dreamer-who-understands-the-dream. The dreamer-who-dreams-the-dream creates the primary process presentation; the dreamer-who-understands-the-dream is the interpreter, the creator of symbolic meanings. Sandler (1976) distinguishes the "dream work" (a primary process mode of thinking) from the unconscious "understanding work" (a higher-order symbolic function). Sandler points out that there would be no point in the dream work if there were not another aspect of the person to understand the disguised dream wish.

Dreaming involves the capacity to transform the static coexistence of opposites seen in primary process thinking into a dialectical relationship of opposites wherein meanings and dream experience[1] are generated. In primary process thinking (resulting in the dream presentation), there is no negation; each pole of a potential contradiction exists independently of the other. The notion of static coexistence of opposites in the unconscious follows directly from Freud's (1915b) observation that there are no negatives in the unconscious. When opposites statically coexist (i.e., before the unconscious thing

---

[1]Pontalis (1972) believes that analysts err in limiting their conception of a dream to its value as the conveyor of symbolic meanings, thus neglecting the centrality of "dream experience," i.e., "the subjective experience of the dreamer dreaming, and the inter-subjective experience of therapy in which the dream is brought to the analyst, both offered and withheld, speaking yet silent" (p. 23).

presentation becomes hypercathected in the process of becoming conscious), no meanings can be generated, since meaning requires difference, a dynamic relationship between an idea and that which it is not. In a completely homogeneous field, there can be no meaning, because the entire field is invisible until it is contrasted with something that it is not.[2]

Dreaming is the process of bringing the dream presentation into a dialectical process, thereby creating the dream experience, i.e., creating meaningful experience where there had only been static coexistence of bits of data. The entry of the dream presentation into a dialectical process involves the transformation of the presentation into symbols that can be understood by an interpreting self. Symbolizing occurs only within the context of a dialectical process, and, conversely, the existence of a dialectical process is manifested by the process of generating symbolic meanings (although it is by no means restricted to the process of generating symbolic meanings).

In the absence of a dialectical process (and therefore in the absence of the capacity for symbolization), the dream presentation, instead of being transformed into a set of symbolic meanings in the process of dreaming, becomes transformed into a hallucination. The schizophrenic, when incapable of maintaining a psychological dialectical process, is consequently incapable of *dreaming* (creating dream experience). It is not, as had been believed, that schizophrenics do not dream; rather, the dream presentation is transformed into a hallucination

[2]Sartre (1943) makes a similar point when he states that there must be a rim of negation (nothingness) around "being-in-itself" in order for reflective consciousness ("being-for-itself") to be generated.

that is subjectively interchangeable with waking hallucinatory experience and therefore is not noticed by the schizophrenic as a unique form of psychological event.

A hospitalized, chronic schizophrenic patient whom I had been seeing five times a week in psychotherapy for several years reported that his roommate had gotten up in the middle of the night and drowned him in a bathtub by holding his head under the water until he was dead. The nursing staff had told me that the patient had slept through the night, so I asked the patient if he had dreamed that. He was surprised that I asked him and looked confused.

Dream experience was so interchangeable with waking experience for this patient that the fact that he was alive and talking to me was not the slightest bit more real to him than what I imagined had been a dream. For him, it was equally possible that current experience was hallucination as it was that his dream experience was real. Even in this case, there is reason to believe that there had been some symbolic reworking of the dream presentation. The fact that the schizophrenic patient created a psychological event that not only could be noticed and remembered, but that also was important enough to communicate to me shows that some reworking of the dream presentation had occurred. The patient transformed the dream presentation into a form of hallucination rather than into a symbolic form. (Despite my suspicion that the hallucination presented by this patient had begun as a dream presentation, it is also possible that the patient's experience of having been drowned was a hallucinatory elaboration of some actual event or may even have been a current hallucination [a hallucinated memory]).

Dreaming occurs for a neurotic patient when he subjects the dream presentation (the thing in itself) to a symbolic transformation. The dream is "dreamed" (is created as a dream experience) at the moment the symbolic transformation occurs, whether that be at the moment an unconscious understanding is achieved in sleep that may only be experienced later as an element in one's waking mood, or whether it occurs at the moment of waking, or at the moment it is "remembered" in an analytic session.

Analytic Space

Analytic space can be thought of as the space between patient and analyst in which analytic experience (including transference illusion) is generated and in which personal meanings can be created and played with. It is a potential space, the existence of which can by no means be taken for granted.

> *Psychotherapy is done in the overlap of the two play areas, that of the patient and that of the therapist.* If the therapist cannot play, then he is not suitable for the work. If the patient cannot play, then something needs to be done to enable the patient to become able to play, after which psychotherapy may begin. (Winnicott, 1971e, p. 54)

(It is beyond the scope of this paper to discuss the problem of working with patients who are unable to play. The present discussion addresses work with patients who are able to participate in the creation and disruption of analytic space.)

Within analytic space, fantasy and reality stand in a

dialectical relationship to each other. The capacity for mature transference (as opposed to delusional transference) involves the capacity to generate an illusion that is experienced simultaneously as real and not real. If the transference experience becomes too real (i.e., if the dialectical relationship collapses in the direction of fantasy), delusional transference is generated. If reality is (defensively) made too present, obsessional intellectualization and concrete operational thinking (Marty and M'Uzan, 1963; McDougall, 1984b) often predominate.

A patient's use of projective identification can be thought of as a collapsing of analytic space in a way that threatens the therapist's capacity to maintain a state of mind in which his own feelings and thoughts can be understood as symbolic constructions as opposed to registrations of fact (Ogden, 1982b). Winnicott (1971e) views projective identification as "direct communication." It is "direct" in the sense that it is communication by means of a direct induction of a feeling state in another person that is not predominantly (and often not at all) mediated by verbal symbols. When the patient is relying heavily on projective identification as a mode of communication, defense, and object-relatedness, the therapist feels locked into a fixed position or sequence of fixed affective states in relation to himself and to the patient. There is such a powerful sense of inevitability about one's feeling state that one does not even consider it to be a subjective state; rather, it is treated as "reality."

The therapist working with borderline and schizophrenic patients must come to accept a degree of unwitting participation in the patient's unconscious object world as an unavoidable avenue to understanding the transference (Ogden, 1979, 1981). When the therapist allows himself to be used in this way, he is *in part* no longer a separate person listening to another person. He has become the "ejected" part of the patient. This part nonetheless continues to be part of the patient, whose psychological perimeter now includes the therapist. In making himself available in this way, the therapist fore-goes his own access to a me/not-me dialectic and becomes the patient *to a degree* in a way that is unmodified by the knowledge that he is not the patient.

When the therapist is serving as the object of a patient's projective identification, the therapist often feels impelled to "do something" about what is happening in-stead of attempting to understand what he is experiencing. When the therapist feels compelled to take action in this way, he is very often exacerbating the collapse of the therapeutic space, the space in which meanings can be understood instead of dispelled.

It is by no means only under the pressure of a pa-tient's projective identifications that the therapist can contribute to the collapse of analytic space. Analytic ther-apy is conducted in the realm of meanings, in the space between symbol and symbolized mediated by the self (as interpreter of one's symbols). Borderline patients charac-teristically operate in the realm of action (as thing in itself); the depressed patient uses self-punishment as a form of activity serving to discharge (the potential for) guilt and thus avoid the experience of guilt (Loewald, 1979); the fetishist freezes potential experience in a thing (fetish object) that excites and substitutes for the expe-rience of being alive with another person: "He [the fetish-ist] steals his own dreams" (Pontalis, 1972, p. 33).

Many borderline patients, for example, cannot sus-pend from their consciousness an immediate awareness of the fact that the analyst is "just a guy trying to earn a buck" and that his patients are his customers. For a patient capable of creating with the analyst an analytic space, the fact that the analyst must be paid for his work can be played with, i.e., used as material for generating transference illusion. One form of playing with this perception is the creation of the transference illusion (e.g., under the sway of a maternal transference) that the analyst would continue seeing the patient whether or not the patient could pay for the meetings. From there perhaps, the idea will be elaborated to include the image of the patient being injured, unable to work, out of money, and yet continuing to be seen by the analyst. Within potential space, this playing with an idea constitutes imagination. Potential space collapses under conditions where the question "What would happen if I weren't paying?" _must_ be answered. Under such conditions, the patient may fail to pay treatment bills for months, forcing the therapist to answer the patient's question concretely. In such a case, imagination (playing with ideas and feelings) has degenerated into an enactment of fantasy in reality (enactment of a set of ideas and feelings that are treated as facts). This is analogous to play disruption in child therapy: because of the patient's anxiety, the intersubjective space in which playing occurs is replaced by real space in which danger can be managed and acted upon.

It is the task of the therapist, through the management of the framework of therapy and through his interpretations, to provide conditions wherein the patient might dare to create personal meanings in a form that he can experience and play with. The therapist working with borderline patients is forever attempting to "pry open" the space between symbol and symbolized, thus creating a field in which meanings exist, where one thing stands for another in a way that can be thought about and understood. Where symbol is indistinguishable from symbol-

ized, each presentation stands only for itself and, therefore, nothing can be understood: each perception is what
it is, and that is all there is to it.

Either through lack of training or under the pressure
of intense countertransference feelings, the therapist may
cease to interpret the symbolic meanings that the patient
is able to create and instead present interventions that
constitute things in themselves, "statements of fact." The
following are examples of such interventions: "I agree
that you did a lousy thing in that instance." "If they don't
pay, you shouldn't work there anymore." "You'll feel
better after a little time has passed." (Of course, there is a
time and place for suggestion, exhortation, and reassur-
ance. I am speaking here about problems arising from
consistent reliance upon such forms of communication
and relatedness.) In these interventions, there is little
space between symbol and symbolized in which to understand meaning. When a therapist regularly intervenes in
this way, the realm of meaning to a large degree is foreclosed to the patient, and acting out on the part of the
patient is likely to follow.

The following are less obtrusive examples of types of
interventions that tend to erode analytic space by stating
"facts" instead of inquiring into the patient's mode of
constructing his personal symbolic meanings.

> A therapist with a patient who as a child had felt
> under pressure to live up to his parent's "shifting and
> impossible expectations" said to the patient, "You
> could never be sure what the standard was and how to
> pass the test."

The therapist's intervention was a statement of an
aspect of the patient's psychic reality, i.e., one way in

which the patient viewed himself and his parents. However, the intervention stated the psychic reality (the patient's view of himself as a child) as a fact rather than as a personal symbolic construction put together and maintained for reasons that can be understood—it was a meaning created by the patient, not a fact discovered by the therapist. The impact of the intervention was to support subtly the patient's defense, which consisted of his seeing himself as a victim of external forces (his parents, teachers, school administrators, and the therapist, none of whom seemed to be able to make up their minds). An alternate way of framing the intervention would have been to say, "It seems that you felt that your parents' standards were constantly shifting so that you didn't know how to satisfy them. You've said that even now you frequently experience things that way."

In offering genetic clarifications and interpretations it is important not to treat the patient's symbolization of his past experience as if it were one and the same with the symbolized, i.e., one and the same with the past experience itself. What is of importance is the way in which the patient constructs his symbolic representation of the past. The past no longer exists and is absolutely irretrievable. The patient in the present creates his own history, i.e., the patient creates symbols representing his conception of his past. It is one of the analytic tasks to understand the patient's reasons for symbolically representing his past in the way that he does. (See Schafer's [1975] conception of the patient's history as an evolving construction, as opposed to a static, discoverable entity.)

"You fail to recognize how self-defeating you are at your job and in your work with me." Alternately, one might say, "I think it scares you to think that it is you who is invested in defeating yourself at your job and with me." In the first instance, the therapist *knows* the patient has been self-defeating and tells the patient he is blinding himself to that fact. In the second version, the therapist is saying that he feels that the patient feels frightened (for reasons that can be understood) of construing (symbolizing) his behavior in a particular way.

A third example:

A female patient has told the therapist that she loves him and has sexual fantasies about him and wishes to have an affair with him. In the next session, she feels disgusting and does not know why. The therapist responds: "My not having a sexual relationship with you has made you feel disgusting for wishing that that could be." Alternately, the therapist might have said, "I think you've taken my not getting involved with you sexually and romantically as evidence that I feel you should not want that and are disgusting if you do wish for that." In the first version, the therapist tells the patient that she feels disgusting as a result of something he has done (i.e., as a result of his not getting involved with her romantically and sexually). This leaves open the possibility that there is inevitability[3] about her response: unrequited sexual

[3]Patients hold powerful convictions regarding inevitability of meaning that must be disentangled by the analyst. For example, analysands often treat it as self-evident that a woman would feel disgusting for being "fat" or that a man would feel ashamed of having a penis that is "too small." Patients evidence considerable resistance to viewing these ideas as personal beliefs that they have constructed for reasons that can be understood.

and romantic wishes make one feel disgusting. In the second, the emphasis is not on the cause-and-effect relationship (one thing inevitably leading to another), but on the patient's interpretation of the meaning of what has transpired.

Analytic space is a frame of mind contributed to by patient and therapist in which a multiplicity of meanings can be entertained and played with. One thought does not "cause" or have direct impact upon another. The subject, through his act of interpretation, mediates between meanings and creates relationships among symbols. Each personal meaning influences the subject's way of constructing and interrelating his symbols and consequently affects his subsequent acts of interpreting experience. This is the hermeneutic equivalent of the cause-and-effect relationship in physical science. When analytic space collapses, the patient becomes imprisoned in the confines of signs connected to one another by a sense of opaque inevitability.

References

Abraham, K. (1924). A short study of the development of the libido, viewed in the light of mental disorders. In *Selected Papers on Psycho-Analysis*, pp. 418–507. London: Hogarth Press, 1927.

Balint, M. (1968). *The Basic Fault*. London: Tavistock.

Bettelheim, B. (1983). *Freud and Man's Soul*. New York: Knopf.

Bibring, E. (1947). The so-called English school of psychoanalysis. *Psychoanalytic Quarterly* 16: 69–93.

Bick, E. (1968). The experience of the skin in early object relations. *International Journal of Psycho-Analysis* 49: 484–486.

Bion, W. R. (1950). The imaginary twin. In *Second Thoughts*, pp. 3–22. New York: Jason Aronson, 1967.

—— (1952). Group dynamics: a review. In *Experiences in Groups*, pp. 141–192. New York: Basic Books, 1959.

—— (1956). Development of schizophrenic thought. In *Second Thoughts*, pp. 36–42. New York: Jason Aronson, 1967.

—— (1957). Differentiation of the psychotic from the non-psychotic personalities. In *Second Thoughts*, pp. 43–64. New York: Jason Aronson, 1967.

—— (1959). Attacks on linking. *International Journal of Psycho-Analysis* 40: 308–315.

—— (1962a). *Learning from Experience.* New York: Basic Books.

—— (1962b). A theory of thinking. In *Second Thoughts*, pp. 110–119. New York: Jason Aronson, 1967.

—— (1963). *Elements of Psycho-Analysis.* In *Seven Servants.* New York: Jason Aronson, 1977.

—— (1967). *Second Thoughts.* New York: Jason Aronson.

Borges, J. L. (1956a). The immortal. In *Labyrinths*, pp. 105–119. New York: New Directions Books, 1964.

—— (1956b). Tlön, Uqbar, Orbis, Tertius. In *Labyrinths*, pp. 3–18. New York: New Directions Books, 1964.

Bornstein, M. (1975). Qualities of color vision in infancy. *Journal of Experimental Child Psychology* 19: 401–419.

Bower, T. G. R. (1971). The object in the world of the infant. *Scientific American* 225: 30–48.

—— (1977). *The Perceptual World of the Child.* Cambridge: Harvard University Press.

Bowlby, J. (1969). *Attachment and Loss.* Vol. 1. New York: Basic Books.

Boyer, L. B. (1967). Historical development of psychoanalytic psychotherapy of the schizophrenias: the followers of Freud. In *Psychoanalytic Treatment of Schizophrenic, Borderline, and Characterological Disorders*, L. B. Boyer and P. L. Giovacchini, pp. 71–128. New York: Jason Aronson.

—— (1983). *The Regressed Patient.* New York: Jason Aronson.

Boyer, L. B., and Giovacchini, P. L. (1967). *Psychoanalytic Treatment of Schizophrenic, Borderline and Characterological Disorders.* New York: Jason Aronson.

Brazelton, T. B. (1981). *On Becoming a Family: The Growth of Attachment.* New York: Delta/Seymour Lawrence.

Brazelton, T. B., and Als, H. (1979). Four early stages in the development of the mother–infant interaction. *Psychoanalytic Study of the Child* 34: 349–369.

Chomsky, N. (1957). *Syntactic Structures*. The Hague: Mouton.
—— (1968). *Language and Mind*. New York: Harcourt, Brace and World.

Eimas, P. (1975). Speech perception in early infancy. In *Infant Perception: From Sensation to Cognition*. Vol. 2, ed, L. B. Cohen and P. Salapatek, pp. 193–228. New York: Academic Press.
Eliade, M. (1963). *Myth and Reality*. New York: Harper & Row.
Erikson, E. (1950). *Childhood and Society*. New York: Norton.

Fain, M. (1971). Prélude à la vie fantasmatique. *Revue Française Psychanalyse* 35: 291–364.
Fairbairn, W. R. D. (1940). Schizoid factors in the personality. In *Psychoanalytic Studies of the Personality*, pp. 3–27. London: Routledge and Kegan Paul, 1952.
—— (1941). A revised psychopathology of the psychoses and psychoneuroses. In *Psychoanalytic Studies of the Personality*, pp. 28–58. London: Routledge and Kegan Paul, 1952.
—— (1944). Endopsychic structure considered in terms of object-relationships. In *Psychoanalytic Studies of the Personality*, pp. 82–136. London: Routledge and Kegan Paul, 1952.
—— (1946).Object-relationships and dynamic structures. In *Psychoanalytic Studies of the Personality*, pp. 137–151. London: Routledge and Kegan Paul, 1952.
—— (1958). On the nature and aims of the psycho-analytical treatment. *International Journal of Psycho-Analysis* 39: 374–385.
Freud, A. (1965). *Normality and Pathology in Childhood: Assessments of Development*. New York: International Universities Press.
Freud, S. (1894). The neuro-psychoses of defence. *S. E.* 3.
—— (1895). Project for a scientific psychology. *S. E.* 1.
—— (1896a). Further remarks on the neuropsychoses of defence. *S. E.* 3.

——— (1896b). Letter to Fliess, December 6, 1896. In *Origins of Psycho-Analysis*, ed. M. Bonaparte, A. Freud, E. Kris, pp. 173–181. New York: Basic Books, 1954.

——— (1900). *The Interpretation of Dreams. S. E.* 4/5.

——— (1905). *Three Essays on the Theory of Sexuality. S. E.* 7.

——— (1911). Formulations on the two principles of mental functioning. *S. E.* 12.

——— (1911–1915). Papers on technique. *S. E.* 12.

——— (1914). On narcissism: an introduction. *S. E.* 14.

——— (1915a). Instincts and their vicissitudes. *S. E.* 14.

——— (1915b). The unconscious. *S. E.* 14.

——— (1916–1917). Introductory lectures on psycho-analysis, XXIII. *S. E.* 15/16.

——— (1917). Mourning and melancholia. *S. E.* 14.

——— (1918). From the history of an infantile neurosis. *S. E.* 17.

——— (1920). *Beyond the Pleasure Principle. S. E.* 18.

——— (1923). *The Ego and the Id. S. E.* 19.

——— (1926). The question of lay analysis. *S. E.* 20.

——— (1927). Fetishism. *S. E.* 21.

——— (1932). New Introductory Lectures XXXI: the dissection of the psychical personality. *S. E.* 22.

——— (1940a). *An Outline of Psycho-Analysis. S. E.* 23.

——— (1940b). Splitting of the ego in the process of defence. *S. E.* 23.

Glover, E. (1945). Examination of the Klein system of child psychology. *Psychoanalytic Study of the Child* 1: 75–118.

——— (1968). *The Birth of the Ego.* New York: International Universities Press.

Green, A. (1975). The analyst, symbolization, and absence in the analytic setting. (On changes in analytic practice and analytic experience). *International Journal of Psycho-Analysis* 56: 1–22.

Greenberg, J., and Mitchell, S. (1983). *Object Relations in Psychoanalytic Theory.* Cambridge: Harvard University Press.

Groddeck, G. (1923). *The Book of the It.* New York: Vintage Books, 1949.

Grotstein, J. (1978). Inner space: its dimensions and its coordinates. *International Journal of Psycho-Analysis* 59: 55–61.

—— (1979a). Demoniacal possession, splitting and the torment of joy. *Contemporary Psychoanalysis* 15: 407–445.

—— (1979b). Who is the dreamer who dreams the dream and who is the dreamer who understands it. *Contemporary Psychoanalysis* 15: 110–169.

—— (1980a). The significance of Kleinian contributions to psychoanalysis. I. Kleinian instinct theory. *International Journal of Psychoanalytic Psychotherapy* 8: 375–392.

—— (1980b). The significance of Kleinian contributions to psychoanalysis. II. Freudian and Kleinian conceptions of early mental development. *International Journal of Psychoanalytic Psychotherapy* 8: 393–428.

—— (1981). *Splitting and Projective Identification.* New York: Jason Aronson.

—— (1983). The Dual Track Theorem. Unpublished manuscript.

—— (1985). A proposed revision for the psychoanalytic concept of the death instinct. *Yearbook of Psychoanalysis and Psychotherapy.* Vol. 1, pp. 299–326. Hillsdale, NJ: New Concept Press.

Habermas, J. (1968). *Knowledge and Human Interests.* Trans. J. Shapiro. Boston: Beacon Press, 1971.

Hartmann, H. (1964). *Essays on Ego Psychology.* New York: International Universities Press.

Hegel, G. W. F. (1807). *Phenomenology of Spirit.* Trans. A. V. Miller. London: Oxford University Press, 1977.

Isaacs, S. (1952). The nature and function of phantasy. In *Developments in Psycho-Analysis*, M. Klein, P. Heimann, S. Isaacs, J. Rivière, pp. 67–121. London: Hogarth Press.

Jacobson, E. (1964). *The Self and the Object World.* New York: International Universities Press.

Jacoby, R. (1983). *The Repression of Psychoanalysis: Otto Fenichel and the Political Freudians.* New York: Basic Books.

Kernberg, O. (1970). A psychoanalytic classification of character pathology. *Journal of the American Psychoanalytic Association* 18: 800–822.

Khan, M. M. R. (1963). The concept of cumulative trauma. *Psychoanalytic Study of the Child* 18: 286–306.

—— (1972). The use and abuse of dream in psychic experience. In *The Privacy of the Self,* pp. 306–315. New York: International Universities Press, 1974.

—— (1979). *Alienation in Perversions.* New York: International Universities Press.

Klein, M. (1928). Early stages of the Oedipus conflict. In *Contributions to Psycho-Analysis, 1921–1945,* pp. 202–214. London: Hogarth Press, 1968.

—— (1930). The importance of symbol-formation in the development of the ego. In *Contributions to Psycho-Analysis, 1921–1945,* pp. 236–250. London: Hogarth Press, 1968.

—— (1932a). The effect of early anxiety situations on the sexual development of the girl. In *The Psycho-Analysis of Children,* pp. 268–325. New York: Humanities Press, 1969.

—— (1932b). *The Psycho-Analysis of Children.* New York: Humanities Press, 1969.

—— (1935). A contribution to the psychogenesis of manic-depressive states. In *Contributions to Psycho-Analysis, 1921–1945,* pp. 282–311. London: Hogarth Press, 1968.

—— (1940). Mourning and its relation to manic-depressive states. In *Contributions to Psycho-Analysis, 1921–1945,* pp. 311–338. London: Hogarth Press, 1968.

—— (1945). The Oedipus complex in the light of early anxieties. In *Contributions to Psycho-Analysis, 1921–1945,* pp. 339–390. London: Hogarth Press, 1968.

—— (1946). Notes on some schizoid mechanisms. In *Envy*

and Gratitude and Other Works, 1946-1963, pp. 1-24. New York: Delacorte, 1975.

—— (1948). On the theory of anxiety and guilt. In *Envy and Gratitude and Other Works, 1946-1963*, pp. 25-42. New York: Delacorte, 1975.

—— (1952a). Mutual influences in the development of ego and id. In *Envy and Gratitude and Other Works, 1946-1963*, pp. 57-60. New York: Delacorte, 1975.

—— (1952b). On observing the behaviour of young infants. In *Envy and Gratitude and Other Works, 1946-1963*, pp. 94-121. New York: Delacorte, 1975.

—— (1952c). Some theoretical conclusions regarding the emotional life of the infant. In *Envy and Gratitude and Other Works, 1946-1963*, pp. 61-93. New York: Delacorte, 1975.

—— (1955). On identification. In *Envy and Gratitude and Other Works, 1946-1963*, pp. 141-175. New York: Delacorte, 1975.

—— (1957). Envy and gratitude. In *Envy and Gratitude and Other Works, 1946-1963*. New York: Delacorte, 1975.

—— (1958). On the development of mental functioning. In *Envy and Gratitude and Other Works, 1946-1963*, pp. 236-246. New York: Delacorte, 1975.

—— (1961). *Narrative of a Child Analysis.* New York: Delacorte, 1975.

—— (1963a). On the sense of loneliness. In *Envy and Gratitude and Other Works, 1946-1963*, pp. 300-313. New York: Delacorte, 1975.

—— (1963b). Some reflections on *The Oresteia.* In *Envy and Gratitude and Other Works, 1946-1963*, pp. 275-299. New York: Delacorte, 1975.

—— (1975). *Envy and Gratitude and Other Works, 1946-1963.* New York: Delacorte.

Klein, M., Heimann, P., Isaacs, S., Rivière, J. (1952). *Developments in Psycho-Analysis.* London: Hogarth Press.

Kojève, A. (1934-1935). *Introduction to the Reading of Hegel.*

Trans. J. H. Nichols, Jr. Ithaca, NY: Cornell University Press, 1969.

Lacan, J. (1949–1960). *Écrits*. Trans. A. Sheridan. New York: W. W. Norton, 1977.
—— (1956a). The Freudian thing or the meaning of the return to Freud in psychoanalysis. In *Écrits*, pp. 114–145. New York: W. W. Norton, 1977.
—— (1956b). The function and field of speech and language in psychoanalysis. In *Écrits*, pp. 30–113. New York: W. W. Norton, 1977.
—— (1957). On a question preliminary to any possible treatment of psychosis. In *Écrits*, pp. 179–225. New York: W. W. Norton, 1977.
—— (1961). The direction of the analysis and the principles of its power. In *Écrits*, pp. 226–280. New York: W. W. Norton, 1977.
Laing, R. D. (1959). *The Divided Self*. Baltimore: Pelican, 1965.
Langs, R. (1976). *The Bipersonal Field*. New York: Jason Aronson.
Lemaire, A. (1970). *Jacques Lacan*. Boston: Routledge and Kegan Paul.
Lewin, B. (1950). *The Psychoanalysis of Elation*. New York: Psychoanalytic Quarterly.
Little, M. (1958). On delusional transference (transference psychosis). *International Journal of Psycho-Analysis* 39: 134–138.
Loewald, H. (1979). The waning of the Oedipus complex. In *Papers on Psychoanalysis*, pp. 384–404. New Haven: Yale University Press, 1980.
Lorenz, K. (1937). *Studies in Animal and Human Behaviour*. Vol. 1. Trans. R. Martin. London: Methuen.

Mackay, N. (1981). Melanie Klein's metapsychology: phenomenological and mechanistic perspectives. *International Journal of Psycho-Analysis* 62: 187–198.
Mahler, M. (1968). *On Human Symbiosis and the Vicissitudes of*

Individuation. Vol. 1. New York: International Universities Press.

Malin, A., and Grotstein, J. (1966). Projective identification in the therapeutic process. *International Journal of Psycho-Analysis* 47: 26–31.

Marty, P., and M'Uzan, M. de (1963). La pensée operatoire. *Revue Française Psychoanalyse* 27: 345–356.

McDougall, J. (1974). The Psychosoma and the Psycho-Analytic Process. *International Review of Psycho-Analysis* 1: 437–459.

―――― (1984a). On psychosomatic vulnerability. *International Journal of Psychiatry in Medicine* 14: 123–131.

―――― (1984b). The disaffected patient: reflections on affect pathology. *Psychoanalytic Quarterly* 53: 386–409.

Meltzer, D. (1975). The psychology of autistic states and of post-autistic mentality. In *Explorations in Autism*, ed. D. Meltzer, J. Bremner, S. Hoxter, D. Weddell, I. Wittenberg, pp. 6–29. London: Clunie Press.

Nemiah, J. (1977). Alexithymia: theoretical considerations. *Psychotherapy and Psychosomatics* 28: 199–206.

Nichols, J. (1960). Translator's Note. In *Introduction to the Reading of Hegel.* Trans. A. Kojève. Ithaca, NY: Cornell University Press, 1969.

Ogden, T. (1974). A psychoanalytic psychotherapy of a patient with cerebral palsy: the relationship of aggression to self and body representations. *International Journal of Psychoanalytic Psychotherapy* 3: 419–433.

―――― (1976). Psychological unevenness in the academically successful student. *International Journal of Psychoanalytic Psychotherapy* 5: 437–448.

―――― (1978). A developmental view of identifications resulting from maternal impingements. *International Journal of Psychoanalytic Psychotherapy* 7: 486–507.

―――― (1979). On projective identification. *International Journal of Psycho-Analysis* 60: 357–373.

―――― (1980). On the nature of schizophrenic conflict. *International Journal of Psycho-Analysis* 61: 513–533.

―――― (1981). Projective identification in psychiatric hospital treatment. *Bulletin of the Menninger Clinic* 45: 317–333.

―――― (1982a). *Projective Identification and Psychotherapeutic Technique*. New York: Jason Aronson.

―――― (1982b). Treatment of the schizophrenic state of nonexperience. In *Technical Factors in the Treatment of the Severely Disturbed Patient*, ed. L. B. Boyer and P. L. Giovacchini, pp. 217–260. New York: Jason Aronson.

―――― (1985). Instinct, structure and personal meaning. *Yearbook of Psychoanalysis and Psychotherapy*. Vol. 1, pp. 327–334. Hillsdale, NJ: New Concept Press.

Piaget, J. (1936). *The Origins of Intelligence in Children*. New York: International Universities Press, 1954.

―――― (1946). *Play, Dreams and Imitation in Childhood*. New York: W. W. Norton, 1962.

―――― (1954). *The Construction of Reality in the Child*. New York: Basic Books.

Pontalis, J.-B. (1972). Between the dream as object and the dream-text. In *Frontiers in Psycho-Analysis*, pp. 23–55. New York: International Universities Press, 1981.

Racker, H. (1957). The meanings and uses of countertransference. *Psychoanalytic Quarterly* 26: 303–357.

Samuels, A. (1983). The theory of archetypes in Jungian and post-Jungian analytical psychology. *International Review of Psycho-Analysis* 10: 429–444.

Sander, L. (1964). Adaptive relations in early mother-child interactions. *Journal of the Academy of Child Psychiatry* 3: 231–264.

―――― (1975). Infant and caretaking environment: investigation and conceptualization of adaptive behaviour in a system of increasing complexity. In *Explorations in Child*

Psychiatry, ed. E. J. Anthony, pp. 129–166. New York: Plenum Press.

Sandler, J. (1976). Dreams, unconscious fantasies and "identity of perception." *International Review of Psycho-Analysis* 3: 33–42.

Sandler, J., and Rosenblatt, B. (1962). The concept of the representational world. *Psychoanalytic Study of the Child* 17: 128–145.

Sartre, J.-P. (1943). *Being and Nothingness*. Trans. H. Barnes. New York: Philosophical Library.

Schafer, R. (1968). *Aspects of Internalization*. New York: International Universities Press.

—— (1975). The psychoanalytic life history. In *Language and Insight*, pp. 3–28. New Haven: Yale University Press.

—— (1976). *A New Language for Psychoanalysis*. New Haven: Yale University Press.

Schmideberg, M. (1935). Discussion, British Psychoanalytical Society, October 16, 1935. Quoted by E. Glover, *Psychoanalytic Study of the Child* 1: 75–118.

Searles, H. (1963). Transference psychosis in the psychotherapy of chronic schizophrenia. In *Collected Papers on Schizophrenia and Related Subjects*, pp. 654–716. New York: International Universities Press.

—— (1972). The function of the patient's realistic perceptions of the analyst in delusional transference. *British Journal of Medical Psychology* 45: 1–18.

—— (1979). Jealousy involving an internal object. In *Advances in Psychotherapy of the Borderline Patient*, ed. J. LeBoit and A. Capponi, pp. 347–404. New York: Jason Aronson.

—— (1982). Some aspects of separation and loss in psychoanalytic therapy with borderline patients. In *Technical Factors in the Treatment of the Severely Disturbed Patient*, ed. L. B. Boyer and P. Giovacchini, pp. 131–160. New York: Jason Aronson.

Segal, H. (1957). Notes on symbol formation. *International Journal of Psycho-Analysis* 38: 391–397.

—— (1964). *An Introduction to the Work of Melanie Klein.* New York: Basic Books.

Sifneos, P. (1972). *Short-Term Psychotherapy and Emotional Crisis.* Cambridge: Harvard University Press.

Spitz, R. (1959). *A Genetic Field Theory of Ego Formation.* New York: International Universities Press.

Stern, D. (1977). *The First Relationship: Infant and Mother.* Cambridge: Harvard University Press.

—— (1983). The early development of schemas of self, other, and "self with other." In *Reflections on Self Psychology*, ed. J. Lichtenberg and S. Kaplan, pp. 49–84. Hillsdale, NJ: Analytic Press.

Tinbergen, N. (1957). On anti-predator response in certain birds: a reply. *Journal of Comparative Physiologic Psychology* 50: 412–414.

Trevarthan, C. (1979). Communication and cooperation in early infancy: a description of primary intersubjectivity. In *Before Speech*, ed. M. Bellowa. Cambridge: Cambridge University Press.

Tustin, F. (1972). *Autism and Childhood Psychosis.* London: Hogarth Press.

Waelder, R. (1937). The problem of the genesis of psychical conflict in early infancy. *International Journal of Psycho-Analysis* 18: 406–473.

Winnicott, D. W. (1945). Primitive emotional development. In *Through Paediatrics to Psycho-Analysis*, pp. 145–156. New York: Basic Books, 1975.

—— (1947). Hate in the countertransference. In *Through Paediatrics to Psycho-Analysis*, pp. 194–203. New York: Basic Books, 1975.

—— (1948). Paediatrics and psychiatry. In *Through Paediatrics to Psycho-Analysis*, pp. 157–173. New York: Basic Books, 1975.

—— (1951). Transitional objects and transitional phenomena. In *Playing and Reality*, pp. 1–25. New York: Basic Books, 1971.

——— (1952). Psychoses and child care. In *Through Paediatrics to Psycho-Analysis*, pp. 219–228. New York: Basic Books, 1975.

——— (1954). Metapsychological and clinical aspects of regression within the psycho-analytical set-up. In *Through Paediatrics to Psycho-Analysis*, pp. 278–294. New York: Basic Books, 1975.

——— (1954–1955). The depressive position in normal development. In *Through Paediatrics to Psycho-Analysis*, pp. 262–277. New York: Basic Books, 1975.

——— (1956). Primary maternal preoccupation. In *Through Paediatrics to Psycho-Analysis*, pp. 300–305. New York: Basic Books, 1975.

——— (1957). "Why do babies cry?" In *The Child, The Family and the Outside World*, pp. 58–68. Baltimore: Penguin Books, 1964.

——— (1958a). Psycho-analysis and the sense of guilt. In *The Maturational Processes and the Facilitating Environment*, pp. 15–28. New York: International Universities Press, 1965.

——— (1958b). The capacity to be alone. In *The Maturational Processes and the Facilitating Environment*, pp. 29–36. New York: International Universities Press, 1965.

——— (1959–64). Classification: is there a psychoanalytical contribution to psychiatric classification? In *The Maturational Processes and the Facilitating Environment*, pp. 124–139. New York: International Universities Press, 1965.

——— (1960a). Ego distortion in terms of true and false self. In *The Maturational Processes and the Facilitating Environment*, pp. 140–152. New York: International Universities Press, 1965.

——— (1960b). The theory of the parent-infant relationship. In *The Maturational Processes and the Facilitating Environment*, pp. 37–55. New York: International Universities Press, 1965.

—— (1962a). A personal view of the Kleinian contribution. In *The Maturational Processes and the Facilitating Environment*, pp. 171-178. New York: International Universities Press, 1965.

—— (1962b). Ego integration in child development. In *The Maturational Processes and the Facilitating Environment*, pp. 56-63. New York: International Universities Press, 1965.

—— (1963). Communicating and not communicating leading to a study of certain opposites. In *The Maturational Processes and the Facilitating Environment*, pp. 179-192. New York: International Universities Press, 1965.

—— (1967a). The location of cultural experience. In *Playing and Reality*, pp. 95-103. New York: Basic Books, 1971.

—— (1967b). Mirror role of mother and family in child development. In *Playing and Reality*, pp. 111-118. New York: Basic Books, 1971.

—— (1968). The use of an object and relating through cross identifications. In *Playing and Reality*, pp. 86-94. New York: Basic Books, 1971.

—— (1971a). Creativity and its origins. In *Playing and Reality*, pp. 65-85. New York: Basic Books.

—— (1971b). Dreaming, fantasying, and living. In *Playing and Reality*, pp. 26-37. New York: Basic Books.

—— (1971c). Playing: a theoretical statement. In *Playing and Reality*, pp. 38-52. New York: Basic Books.

—— (1971d). Playing: creative activity and the search for the self. In *Playing and Reality*, pp. 53-64. New York: Basic Books.

—— (1971e). *Playing and Reality*. New York: Basic Books.

—— (1971f). The place where we live. In *Playing and Reality*, pp. 104-110. New York: Basic Books.

Zetzel, E. (1956). An approach to the relation between concept and content in psychoanalytic theory (with special reference to the work of Melanie Klein and her followers). *Psychoanalytic Study of the Child* 11: 99-121.

Index

Externality, discovery of,
   survival of object and,
   190–197

Fain, M., 184–185
Fairbairn, W. R. D., 2, 4, 6,
   10, 54, 102, 133, 136,
   144, 145, 150, 163, 164
   and internal objects, 147–
   148
   and object relations theory
   of internal objects, 139–
   143
   and resistance, 155–156
   on theoretical status of
   internal objects, 140–
   141
False Self, 143–144, 178
Fantasy. *See also* Phantasy
   dissociation of reality and,
   222
   foreclosure of reality and,
   222–224
   reality as defense against,
   219–221
   reality subsumed by, 216–
   219
Fantasy activity, early. *See*
   Early fantasy activity
"Fetishism," 135
Foreclosure, of reality and
   fantasy, 222–224
Freud, A., 68, 167, 174
Freud, S., 4–5, 6–7, 11, 12,
   16, 34–35, 67, 82, 92,
   102, 118, 133, 136, 137,

138, 139, 140, 141, 142,
147, 149, 150, 157, 164,
168, 171, 174, 176, 179,
208, 210, 222, 235
on active agency, 134–135
and hallucinatory wish
   fulfillment, 179
and "inheritance of
   knowledge," 18–23
and object relations theory
   of internal objects, 133–
   136
on sexual meanings, 20–21

Giovacchini, P. L., 112
Glover, E., 68, 94, 168
"Good enough" mother, 140
Green, A., 223
Greenberg, J., 19
Grotstein, J., 15, 16, 29, 32,
   43, 44, 47, 182, 193,
   211, 213, 223, 235
   dual track model of, 147
Guilt, and benign circle, ruth
   and, 197–200
Guntrip, H., 10

Habermas, J., 73
Hartmann, H., 132
Hegel, G. W. F., 61, 208
Heimann, P., 28
Historical position, 82
Historical subject, birth of,
   depressive position and,
   67–99
History